BIBLE
PROPHECIES

FAITH, HISTORY & HOPE

PUBLISHER

Richard Fraiman

GENERAL MANAGER

Steven Sandonato

EXECUTIVE DIRECTOR, MARKETING SERVICES

Carol Pittard

DIRECTOR, RETAIL & SPECIAL SALES

Tom Mifsud

DIRECTOR, NEW PRODUCT DEVELOPMENT

Peter Harper

ASSISTANT DIRECTOR, NEWSSTAND MARKETING

Laura Adam

ASSISTANT DIRECTOR, BRAND MARKETING

Joy Butts

ASSOCIATE COUNSEL

Helen Wan

SENIOR BRAND MANAGER, TWRS/M

Holly Oakes

BRAND & LICENSING MANAGER

Alexandra Bliss

DESIGN & PREPRESS MANAGER

Anne-Michelle Gallero

BOOK PRODUCTION MANAGER

Susan Chodakiewicz

GENERAL EDITOR

Christopher D. Hudson

SENIOR EDITOR

Kelly Knauer

MANAGING EDITOR

Carol Smith

CONSULTING EDITORS FROM THE AMERICAN BIBLE SOCIETY'S NIDA INSTITUTE FOR BIBLICAL SCHOLARSHIP:

Barbara Bernstengel

Robert Hodgson, Ph.D.

Charles Houser

WITH SPECIAL THANKS TO THE AMERICAN BIBLE SOCIETY'S COMMITTEE ON TRANSLATION AND SCHOLARSHIP

CONTRIBUTING WRITERS

Elizabeth Arlene

Laura Coggin

Benjamin D. Irwin

Carol Smith

DESIGN AND PRODUCTION

Symbology Creative

Mark Wainwright

SPECIAL THANKS:

Glenn Buonocore

Tymothy Byers

Margaret Hess

Suzanne Janso

Brynn Joyce

Robert Marasco

Brooke Reger

Mary Sarro-Waite

Ilene Schreider

Adriana Tierno

Alex Voznesenskiy

© 2009 Time Inc. Home Entertainment

Time Inc.

1271 Avenue of the Americas

New York, New York 10020

ISBN 10: 1-60320-068-1

ISBN 13: 978-1-60320-068-4

Library of Congress Number: 2008909721

We welcome your comments and suggestions about Bible Prophecies. Please write to us at:

Bible Prophecies

Attention: Book Editors

PO Box 11016

Des Moines, IA 50336-1016

If you would like to order any of our hardcover Collector's Edition books, please call us at 1-800-327-6388.

(Monday through Friday, 7:00 a.m.–8:00 p.m. or Saturday, 7:00 a.m.– 6:00 p.m. Central Time).

BIBLE PROPHECIES

FAITH, HISTORY & HOPE

TABLE OF CONTENTS

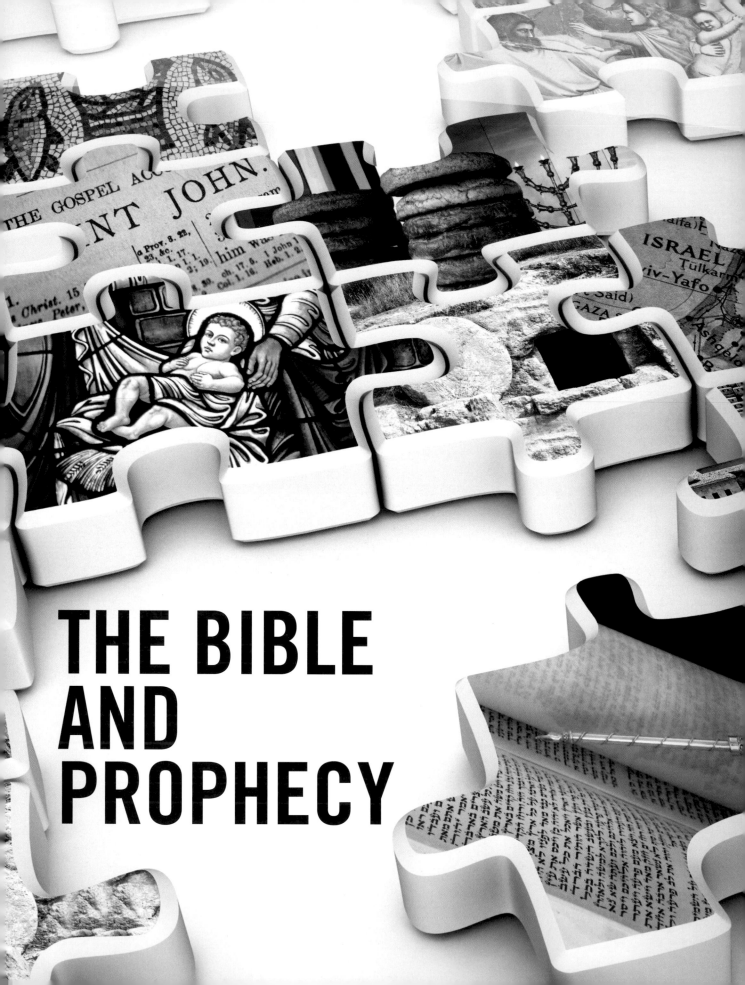

THE BIBLE
AND
PROPHECY

THE BIBLE REVEALS AN ANCIENT WORLD SHAPED BY KINGS, WARRIORS, AND PROPHETS.

AND WHILE KINGS AND WARRIORS COLLECTED THE GLORY AND SPOILS OF WAR, PROPHETS WERE OFTEN THE MOST FEARED AND INFLUENTIAL OF THEM ALL. SOMETIMES UNDERSTOOD TO BE MERE FORECASTERS OF THE FUTURE, PROPHETS, IN FACT, ADVISED KINGS AND EXHORTED NATIONS. PROPHETS SPOKE FOR GOD. THEY ENCOURAGED, REPRIMANDED, AND SHARED GOD'S MESSAGE WITH THOSE WHO WOULD LISTEN—AND SOMETIMES WITH THOSE WHO WOULD NOT.

Some prophets spoke. Others wrote. Some communicated through dramatic public acts, like shaving their heads or calling down fire from heaven. Their methods ranged from the conventional to the bizarre. Their messages contained themes of both terrifying judgment and unwavering hope, sometimes in practically the same breath.

Like the men (and a few women) who delivered them, biblical prophecies took many forms. Some prophecies pointed to future events. For example, the prophet Elijah predicted the gruesome death that awaited Israel's Queen Jezebel (1 Kings 21:23). Another prophet named Daniel informed the Babylonian king of his empire's pending collapse (Daniel 5). More often, though, prophets warned people about what would happen if they stopped obeying God's laws and did not turn back to God. Because the prophets used a variety of symbolic language and imagery, their messages can be interpreted in many ways.

People in the ancient world turned to dreams, visions, and natural phenomena, hoping to uncover a message from God—a message interpreted and announced to the people by a prophet.

Perhaps the most famous biblical prophecies are the apocalyptic passages found in books like Daniel and Revelation. Some Bible interpreters believe passages such as those found in books like Daniel and Revelation describe events still to come, and they read their Bibles alongside today's headlines, looking for the fulfillment of visions recorded in these books.

SHAPING THE HISTORY OF ISRAEL

The prophets of the Bible are intertwined with the history of Israel.

Hebrew culture began with the patriarchs: Abraham, Isaac, and Jacob. As their nomadic descendants settled in the promised land, national champions known as "judges" rose up to administer justice and provide protection from outside enemies. Eventually the Israelites, as they came to be known, established a monarchy, elevating their status in the region.

Prophets played an important role at every stage of Israel's development. At times, they simply communicated God's truth to the people, as Moses did, reminding them not to worship idols or admonishing them to care for the poor. At other times, prophets warned the people of coming judgment. And whether they served as insiders who were among royal advisors or as outsiders protesting against a corrupt establishment, these spokespersons for God urged the nation to remain true to God's instructions.

THE OLD TESTAMENT PROPHET MICAH EXHORTS THE ISRAELITES TO RETURN TO COMPLETE OBEDIENCE TO THE LAWS OF MOSES.

REVEALED OVER TIME

Some prophecies were cloaked in mystery, their full meaning made evident only after their fulfillment.

A PROPHET SPEAKS FOR GOD AND IS CHOSEN BY GOD TO SPEAK TO PEOPLE ON HIS BEHALF AND CONVEY A MESSAGE, TEACHING, OR WARNING.

The Old Testament prophets often spoke of a Messiah, a divinely anointed deliverer who would come to save God's people. While these prophecies may have been understood differently by the first people who heard them, those writing about Jesus years later interpreted them as foretelling his coming: for example, his birth in Bethlehem (Micah 5:2), his sacrificial death as a silent lamb (Isaiah 53:7), his clothes being gambled for by his oppressors (Psalm 22:18). Here are some of these prophecies:

OLD TESTAMENT PROPHECY
Bethlehem Ephrath, you are one of the smallest towns in the nation of Judah. But the LORD will choose one of your people to rule the nation—someone whose family goes back to ancient times. (Micah 5:2)

NEW TESTAMENT PARALLEL
When Jesus was born in the village of Bethlehem in Judea, Herod was king. (Matthew 2:1)

OLD TESTAMENT PROPHECY
He was painfully abused, but he did not complain. He was silent like a lamb being led to the butcher, as quiet as a sheep having its wool cut off. (Isaiah 53:7)

NEW TESTAMENT PARALLEL

The men who were guarding Jesus made fun of him and beat him. They put a blindfold on him and said, "Tell us who struck you!" They kept on insulting Jesus in many other ways. (Luke 22:63–65)

OLD TESTAMENT PROPHECY

They took my clothes and gambled for them. (Psalm 22:18)

NEW TESTAMENT PARALLEL

After the soldiers had nailed Jesus to the cross, they divided up his clothes into four parts, one for each of them. But his outer garment was made from a single piece of cloth, and it did not have any seams. The soldiers said to each other, "Let's not rip it apart. We will gamble to see who gets it." This happened so that the Scriptures would come true, which say,

> *"They divided up my clothes and gambled for my garments."*

The soldiers then did what they had decided. (John 19:23–24)

Entry into Jerusalem, 1308–11
Duccio Di Buoninsegna

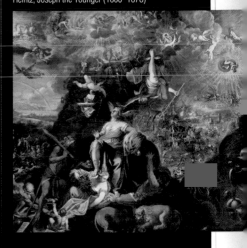

PROPHETS OF ALL KINDS

Generally, biblical prophecies fit into one of three categories.

1.

PROPHECIES ABOUT ISRAEL (AND HER ENEMIES AND ALLIES)

Much of Israel's history revolves around a covenant that God made with the patriarch Abraham, promising his descendants blessing and security if they obeyed God. Victory over enemies was a significant part of this blessing. As a result, many prophetic books condemn the hostile nations that surrounded Israel. At the same time, the prophets also warned that God would use some of these same enemies to punish Israel if the people disobeyed him.

2.

PROPHECIES ABOUT THE MESSIAH

These prophecies promised a remedy to oppression and an antidote for sin: a Messiah or an "Anointed One" who would reverse the effects of the Fall. (This term refers to the events of Genesis 3, when people chose to disobey God and thus lost intimacy with him and harmony with the world.) The Christian faith is based on a belief that Jesus is the fulfillment of this promise.

3.

PROPHECIES ABOUT THE FINAL JUDGMENT OF THE WORLD

These are often referred to as "apocalyptic," and are, by their very nature, symbolic and colorful. The book of Revelation contains some of the best-known statements about the way human history will end and the day of the Lord's return, delivered in a series of dreamlike visions that speak of a final settling of accounts, when God conquers evil and establishes a perfect, glorious kingdom on earth. While these visions may be confusing and at times frightening, they offer hope, reminding us that God rewards those who have persistent faith in him.

■ *When we told you about the power and the return of our Lord Jesus Christ, we were not telling clever stories someone had made up. But with our own eyes we saw his true greatness. . . .*

All of this makes us even more certain that what the prophets said is true. So you should pay close attention to their message, as you would to a lamp shining in some dark place. You must keep on paying attention until daylight comes and the morning star rises in your hearts. But you need to realize that no one alone can understand any of the prophecies in the Scriptures. The prophets did not think these things up on their own, but they were guided by the Spirit of God. 2 Peter 1:16, 19–21

THE TEST OF A TRUE PROPHET

Moses was Israel's national deliverer: He led the people out of slavery in Egypt and organized the system of priests and sacrifices that was central to Jewish religious practice. As Israel's chief lawgiver, he also defined the role of a prophet:

Moses said to Israel:
"You were asking for a prophet the day you were gathered at Mount Sinai and said to the Lord*, 'Please don't let us hear your voice or see this terrible fire again—if we do, we will die!' Then the* Lord *told me:*
Moses, they have said the right thing. So when I want to speak to them, I will choose one of them to be a prophet like you. I will give my message to that prophet, who will tell the people exactly what I have said. Since the message comes from me, anyone who doesn't obey the message will have to answer to me. . . .
You may be asking yourselves, 'How can we tell if a prophet's message really comes from the Lord*?' You will know, because if the* Lord *says something will happen, it will happen. And if it doesn't, you will know that the prophet was falsely claiming to speak for the* Lord*. Don't be afraid of any prophet whose message doesn't come from the* Lord*."*

DEUTERONOMY 18:16–22

WHO'S WHO

Seventeen of the Old Testament's books are considered prophetic, though many of the historical writings contain sections of prophecy as well.

To the right, you'll find the Bible's table of contents, which contains books often referred to as the "major prophets"—Isaiah, Jeremiah and Ezekiel, for example. There is also a group of "minor prophets." This term refers to the size, not the significance, of the books in this section. The original Hebrew writings of the twelve minor prophets could easily fit on one scroll.

You'll also find stories about prophets in books not considered strictly prophetic writings. For example, 1 and 2 Kings contain the stories of two of the greatest Old Testament prophets, Elijah and Elisha. In the book of Exodus (15:20), Miriam, the sister of Moses and Aaron, is the first woman named in the Bible as a prophet. Deborah, a leader of Israel during the days of the judges, was also a prophet (Judges 4:4). Another prophet, Anna, lived at the temple during the time of Jesus' birth. The New Testament Gospel according to Luke records part of her story.

PENTATEUCH
GENESIS
EXODUS
LEVITICUS
NUMBERS
DEUTERONOMY

HISTORICAL BOOKS
JOSHUA
JUDGES
RUTH
1 SAMUEL
2 SAMUEL
1 KINGS
2 KINGS
1 CHRONICLES
2 CHRONICLES
EZRA
NEHEMIAH
ESTHER

POETIC BOOKS
JOB
PSALMS
PROVERBS
ECCLESIASTES
SONG OF SONGS

PROPHETIC BOOKS
MAJOR PROPHETS:
ISAIAH
JEREMIAH
LAMENTATIONS
EZEKIEL
DANIEL*
MINOR PROPHETS:
HOSEA
JOEL
AMOS
OBADIAH
JONAH
MICAH
NAHUM
HABAKKUK
ZEPHANIAH
HAGGAI
ZECHARIAH
MALACHI

*The book of Daniel is considered apocalyptic though Daniel is considered one of the prophets.

NOT CRYSTAL BALLS AND TEA LEAVES

BIBLICAL PROPHECY IS NOT THE CHRISTIAN EQUIVALENT OF ASTROLOGY OR FORTUNE-TELLING, NOR IS IT MERELY AN ATTEMPT TO DIVINE THE FUTURE.

In our modern world, shaped by technology and founded on empirical evidence, the role of a prophet may seem strange, even mystical. However, biblical prophecy is not the Christian equivalent of astrology or fortune-telling, nor is it merely an attempt to divine the future. The prophet's main objective was spiritual: to inspire people to put their trust in God for the future. The most famous biblical prophecies don't just reveal events ahead of time; they remind us of God's control over those events.

The prophecies of the Bible always reveal something about God's plan for the world. Many Old Testament prophecies described God's judgment and restoration of his people. The prophecies concerning a suffering servant and savior supported Jesus' claims to be the Messiah. Apocalyptic literature about the end of human history reminds readers of the final judgment and kindles hope in anticipation of God's new creation.

"Soon you will go into the land that the Lord your God is giving you. The nations that live there do things that are disgusting to the Lord, and you must not follow their example. Don't sacrifice your son or daughter. And don't try to use any kind of magic or witchcraft to tell fortunes or to cast spells or to talk with spirits of the dead. The Lord is disgusted with anyone who does these things, and that's why he will help you destroy the nations that are in the land."
DEUTERONOMY 18:9–12

■ PROPHECY CAN INSPIRE AND INFORM US TO LIVE EACH DAY WITH CONFIDENT ANTICIPATION AS GOD'S REVELATIONS CONTINUE TO UNFOLD. LIVES CAN CHANGE WHEN PEOPLE TRUST THAT GOD'S PLAN IS IN PLACE AND THAT THEY HAVE BEEN EMPOWERED TO BE ENJOINED TO GOD'S MISSION IN CARRYING OUT THAT PLAN. IN THE END, THAT IS THE CENTRAL, REDEEMING MESSAGE BEHIND THE PROPHECIES OF THE BIBLE.

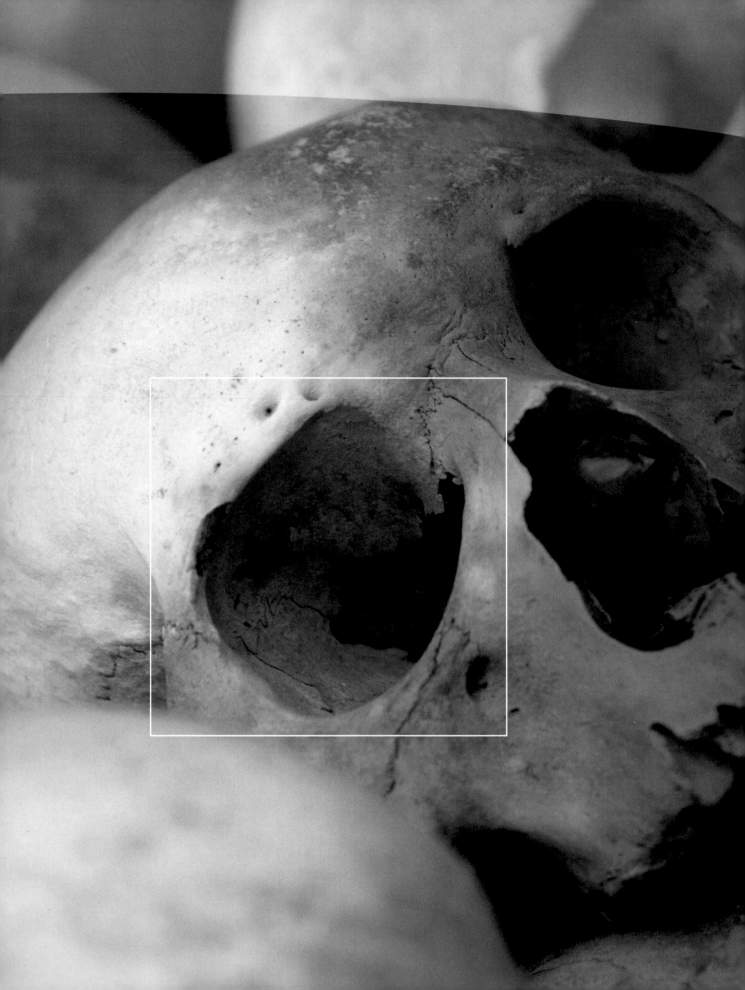

2

ANCIENT PROPHECIES FULFILLED CONCERNING:

ISRAEL

HE THEN TOLD ME TO SAY: "DRY BONES, LISTEN TO WHAT THE LORD IS SAYING TO YOU, 'I, THE LORD GOD, WILL PUT BREATH IN YOU, AND ONCE AGAIN YOU WILL LIVE. I WILL WRAP YOU WITH MUSCLES AND SKIN AND BREATHE LIFE INTO YOU. THEN YOU WILL KNOW THAT I AM THE LORD.'"

EZEKIEL 37:4–6

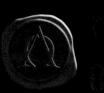

THE BLESSING OF OBEDIENCE

THE ANCIENT NATION OF ISRAEL AND ITS ROLLER-COASTER HISTORY ARE THE FOCUS OF THE OLD TESTAMENT. THE ISRAELITES WERE A PEOPLE DESCENDED FROM ABRAHAM, LIBERATED FROM SLAVERY IN EGYPT, LED INTO THE PROMISED LAND, AND MADE INTO A UNITED NATION THAT WORSHIPED THE ONE TRUE GOD. EVENTUALLY, ISRAEL DIVIDED IN TWO, FORMING NORTHERN AND SOUTHERN KINGDOMS. THEN, ONE AFTER THE OTHER, BOTH KINGDOMS FELL, CONQUERED BY NEIGHBORING EMPIRES.

Throughout its history, prophets reminded the people of Israel of the covenant (agreement) God had made with their ancestors. Blessing and prosperity had been promised in return for obedience to God, they warned, but disobedience would bring ruin. The prophets' words—both for good and for ill—rang true in the story of Israel.

As one prophet after another warned of the price to be paid for ignoring God's laws, they also held out the hope of forgiveness and the restoration of divine grace if the people would change course and renew their relationship with God.

Unfortunately, the people of Israel learned the hard way that without God's protection, the threat of invasion, military occupation, and exile was constant. In this, the prophets were proved right time and again.

"I WILL BLESS YOU AND MAKE YOUR DESCENDANTS INTO A GREAT NATION. YOU WILL BECOME FAMOUS AND BE A BLESSING TO OTHERS. I WILL BLESS THOSE WHO BLESS YOU, BUT I WILL PUT A CURSE ON ANYONE WHO PUTS A CURSE ON

THE PROMISE TO ABRAHAM

The Beginning of the Jewish People

In the first book of the Bible, God spoke to a man from Ur in Chaldea named Abram (later renamed Abraham, meaning "father of many"). Abram was so moved by this divine encounter that he packed up his family and left the home of his ancestors in Ur near the Persian Gulf, following God to the unfamiliar land of Canaan.

Why? Because God promised to bless Abram beyond his wildest dreams. *"I will bless you and make your descendants into a great nation. You will become famous and be a blessing to others. I will bless those who bless you, but I will put a curse on anyone who puts a curse on you. Everyone on earth will be blessed because of you"* (Genesis 12:2–3).

Yet there was a paradox in God's promise. In order to be the "father of many," one must have children —but Abraham and his wife Sarah had been unable to conceive (Genesis 15:2). So God made another promise to Abraham: *"I will bless [Sarah], and you will have a son by her"* (Genesis 17:16). This promise came true in miraculous fashion, when Abraham, then 100 years old, and Sarah, 90, were blessed with a son, Isaac (Genesis 21:1–6).

Isaac was the first and only child of Abraham and Sarah. Later he also became the father of Jacob, whose twelve sons became the heads of twelve tribes that came to be known as Israel. This was the fulfillment of God's promise to Abraham (Genesis 35:23–26).

THROUGH ISAAC

Though Isaac was Abraham and Sarah's only child together, he was not the only son of Abraham.

Because Abraham and Sarah were childless and quite old when God promised to give them a child, they could not envision how that divine pledge would be kept. Taking matters into their own hands, Sarah suggested that Abraham have a baby with her servant Hagar (Genesis 16), who would act as a surrogate mother for her. When the child was born, Abraham and Sarah adopted the baby and named him Ishmael.

Though this practice was culturally acceptable, God had indeed planned a son for Sarah, who eventually became pregnant herself. And once she gave birth to Isaac, the blended family was filled with conflict and resentment until Abraham's death (Genesis 25:7-10).

After Sarah died, Abraham also had six additional sons by a second wife, Keturah (Genesis 25:1-6). While Abraham's inheritance went solely to Isaac, he provided for his other sons while he was living.

In a sense, the family conflict of Abraham, Isaac, Ishmael, and the others continues to this day. The people of Israel believe their ancestry traces back to Isaac (whom they refer to as the promised child), while many Arab people, including Palestinians, trace their heritage to Ishmael, Abraham's firstborn.

Vernet, Horace (1789–1863)
Abraham sends Hagar away, 1837

"THE LORD SAID TO ABRAM: LOOK AROUND TO THE NORTH, SOUTH, EAST, AND WEST. I WILL GIVE YOU AND YOUR FAMILY ALL THE LAND YOU CAN SEE. IT WILL BE THEIRS FOREVER! I WILL GIVE YOU MORE DESCENDANTS THAN THERE ARE SPECKS OF DUST ON THE EARTH, AND SOMEDAY IT WILL BE EASIER TO COUNT THOSE SPECKS OF DUST THAN TO COUNT YOUR DESCENDANTS. NOW WALK BACK AND FORTH ACROSS THE LAND, BECAUSE I AM GOING TO GIVE IT TO YOU." GENESIS 13:14B–17

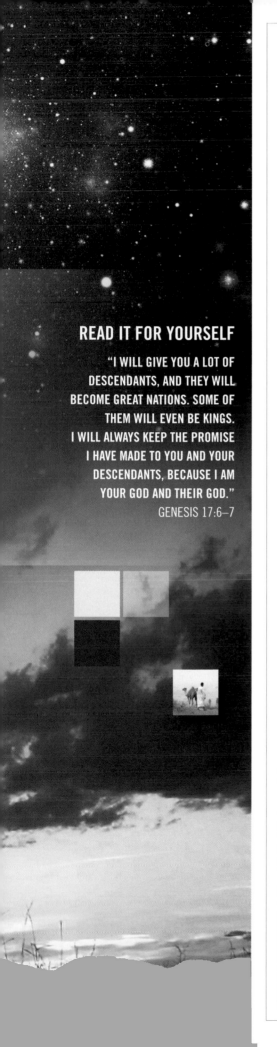

BALAAM AND THE TALKING DONKEY

God kept his promise to make Abraham's descendants a great nation, but the way into the promised land was anything but easy. After Moses led the Israelites out of slavery in Egypt, they began the arduous journey to Canaan, the land God had promised them. The trek brought the Israelites into close proximity with hostile peoples like the Moabites. Balak, king of Moab, didn't like the idea of a large group marching along his border, so he hired a prophet named Balaam to put a curse on the nation.

Unfortunately for Balak, the prophet Balaam spoke only what God told him to say–three blessings for Israel and a warning about what would happen to Moab.

What happened? According to the book of Numbers, on his way to curse the Israelites, Balaam encountered an angel of the LORD. At first, only Balaam's donkey saw the angel and halted. Balaam had places to be, so he started beating his donkey—at which point the donkey spoke up. "What have I done?" it asked (Numbers 22:28). Only then did Balaam see the angel, who ordered Balaam to speak only what God wanted him to say.

Balaam's first three prophecies (Numbers 23:7–24:14) described God's covenant with Abraham and how it would come to fruition through the patriarch's countless descendants, the inheritance of the promised land, and God's blessing on both. God had already said that Abraham's descendants would multiply and fill the earth (Genesis 12:2–3), and in Balaam's first prophecy, he announced that this process was already underway.

Balaam's fourth prophecy (Numbers 24:15–25) listed the nations that Israel would defeat (see 1 Samuel 15:8; 2 Samuel 8:1–14; 1 Chronicles 4:42–43). Bad news for Balak—one of those nations was Moab.

The prophets of God—including such unlikely characters as Balaam—testified that the Israelites would overcome adversity, defeat their enemies, and prosper in the land God was giving them. Much of what follows in the Old Testament traces the fulfillment of these promises.

ISRAEL IS CONQUERED BY ENEMIES

The Great Split

THE ASSYRIAN CONQUEST

Israel's good times were not to last. Just two generations after the death of David, its greatest king, Israel split in two.

Both northern and southern kingdoms wandered away from the covenant forged in the desert between God and Moses following the Exodus. Courageous prophets spoke words of warning to kings and commoners alike, condemning the immorality of God's chosen people: their rampant idolatry, their exploitation of the poor, and their other social ills.

More ominously, the prophets' words revealed the judgment that awaited the two nations. This judgment would come in the form of conquerors from the east—the Assyrians and the Babylonians.

The prophet Isaiah proclaimed these words from God: *"I am furious! And I will use the king of Assyria as a club to beat down you godless people"* (Isaiah 10:5–6). Isaiah continued by prophesying the following words from the king of Assyria: *"I will destroy Jerusalem, together with its gods and idols, just as I did Samaria"* (Isaiah 10:11). A few chapters later, in Isaiah 36, the prophet described the Assyrian attack on Jerusalem, the capital of Judah, the southern kingdom.

The Bible recalls the fulfillment of this daunting prophecy in two other places as well: 2 Kings 18:13–37 and 2 Chronicles 32:1–19. Both of these historical books detail generations of Israelite victories, defeats, misdeeds, and rulers.

Assyria attacked both the northern and southern kingdoms of Israel. The first attack came during the rule of Tiglath Pileser (2 Kings 15:19–20), the second during King Shalmaneser's reign. It was the second attack that resulted in the destruction of Samaria, capital of the northern kingdom (2 Kings 17:5–6). The final Assyrian invasion of Jerusalem, capital of the southern kingdom, is described in 2 Kings 18:13–37 and 2 Chronicles 32:1–19.

By the end of Sennacherib's rule, Isaiah's prophecy had come true. Assyria had wreaked havoc on both kingdoms of Israel.

Assyrian Fresco

READ IT FOR YOURSELF

"THE ASSYRIAN KING TOOK THE ISRAEL-ITES AWAY TO ASSYRIA AS PRISONERS. HE FORCED SOME OF THEM TO LIVE IN THE TOWN OF HALAH, OTHERS TO LIVE NEAR THE HABOR RIVER IN THE TERRITORY OF GOZAN, AND STILL OTHERS TO LIVE IN TOWNS WHERE THE MEDIAN PEOPLE LIVED."   2 KINGS 17:6

Depiction of Adad, the bull storm god, on a Babylonian city wall.

NEBUCHADNEZZAR CONQUERS JERUSALEM

Assyria Proved to Be the Least of the Israelites' Troubles.

By the late 600s BC, Babylonia had grown into one of the world's dominant empires. Its king, Nebuchadnezzar, conquered Jerusalem in 586 BC—just as the prophets Isaiah and Jeremiah had warned.

More than a century before Jerusalem's fall, Isaiah warned Hezekiah, king of Judah, about the city's fate. *"I have a message for you from the LORD All-Powerful,"* Isaiah told the king. *"One day everything you and your ancestors have stored up will be taken to Babylonia. The LORD has promised that nothing will be left. Some of your own sons will be taken to Babylonia, where they will be disgraced and made to serve in the king's palace"* (Isaiah 39:5–7).

Jeremiah painted much the same picture, but he added one crucial detail: the number of years the Israelites would spend in exile. *"This country will be as empty as a desert, because I will make all of you the slaves of the king of Babylonia for 70 years"* (Jeremiah 25:11).

According to the writer of 2 Kings, the Babylonian assault on Jerusalem began around 605 BC, with the final invasion toppling the city almost twenty years later (2 Kings 24:1,10; 25:1).

The writer of 2 Chronicles also recounted Jerusalem's fall to Babylonia: *"In the spring of the year, King Nebuchadnezzar of Babylonia had Jehoiachin arrested and taken to Babylon along with more of the valuable items in the temple. Then Nebuchadnezzar appointed Zedekiah king of Judah"* (2 Chronicles 36:10). The events Isaiah and Jeremiah foretold, including the looting and destruction of the temple and the exile of King Hezekiah's descendants, had come to pass.

READ IT FOR YOURSELF

"A TIME IS COMING WHEN THE SURVIVORS FROM ISRAEL AND JUDAH WILL COMPLETELY DEPEND ON THE HOLY LORD OF ISRAEL, INSTEAD OF THE NATION THAT DEFEATED THEM. THERE WERE AS MANY PEOPLE AS THERE ARE GRAINS OF SAND ALONG THE SEASHORE, BUT ONLY A FEW WILL SURVIVE TO COME BACK TO ISRAEL'S MIGHTY GOD. THIS IS BECAUSE HE HAS THREATENED TO DESTROY THEIR NATION, JUST AS THEY DESERVE. THE LORD ALL-POWERFUL HAS PROMISED THAT EVERYONE ON THIS EARTH WILL BE PUNISHED. NOW THE LORD GOD ALL-POWERFUL SAYS TO HIS PEOPLE IN JERUSALEM:

THE ASSYRIANS WILL BEAT YOU WITH STICKS AND ABUSE YOU, JUST AS THE EGYPTIANS DID. BUT DON'T BE AFRAID OF THEM. SOON I WILL STOP BEING ANGRY WITH YOU, AND I WILL PUNISH THEM FOR THEIR CRIMES."

ISAIAH 10:20–25

NAHUM

The Assyrian empire stood at the peak of its power when Nahum prophesied in Judah—a fact that makes the Old Testament writings attributed to him even more remarkable. They were a prophecy against Assyria and its capital, Nineveh, the leading superpower of Nahum's day.

Nahum was not interested in simply pronouncing bad tidings on Assyria. His was a message about God's power, which Nahum believed was even greater than that of Assyria. Nahum offered hope for the people of Judah, a promise that the God they worshiped was greater than their enemy to the east.

Detail from the Code of Hammurabi stela, which lists Babylonian laws (circa 1760 BC).

THE EXILE OF GOD'S PEOPLE

"To the Victor Go the Spoils"

The prophet Amos mournes over Jerusalem

BIBLE PROPHECIES

In ancient times, the spoils of war often included the very people who had been conquered. They were deported to the victorious country, where they were likely to be enslaved. In the meantime, foreigners would move into the homes and cities vacated by the exiles. This is precisely what happened when Assyria and Babylonia conquered the northern and southern kingdoms of Israel and Judah, respectively (see 2 Kings 17:24).

The first large-scale exile of Israelites happened around 734 BC, when the Assyrian king Tiglath Pileser attacked the northern kingdom (2 Kings 15:29). A second exile to Assyria took place just twelve years later (2 Kings 17:1-6).

After controlling the capital city of Samaria for three years, Assyrian forces overturned the city completely and sent the inhabitants into exile. The Bible simply reads, *"The Assyrian king took the Israelites away to Assyria as prisoners"* (2 Kings 17:6; see also 2 Kings 18:11).

The prophet Amos had warned Israel of a threat to their nation, and it is widely believed he was referring specifically to the Assyrian conquest. Two of the prophet's proclamations in particular seem to describe the deportations from Samaria: *"You may be brave and strong, but you will run away, stripped naked"* (Amos 2:16). *"Enemies will break through their defenses and steal their treasures. The Lord has promised that only a few from Samaria will escape with their lives . . ."* (Amos 3:11-12; see also 2 Kings 10:1-14; Hosea 1:4-5).

The southern kingdom suffered the same fate, from a different conqueror—the Babylonian empire invaded Judah three different times, each leading to exile of the people. These deportations, which took place in 605, 598, and 586 BC, are recorded in 2 Kings 24:1-7, 10-16, and 25:8-21.

Just as the Old Testament prophets spoke prophecies that were directed to the Assyrian exiles, they also foretold the Babylonian exiles. The prophet Micah, for example, warned the parents of Judah: *"Judah, shave your head as bald as a vulture and start mourning. Your precious children will be dragged off to a foreign country"* (Micah 1:16).

The prophet Isaiah also had words for Judah: *Then I asked the Lord, 'How long will this last?' The Lord answered: Until their towns are destroyed and their houses are deserted, until their fields are empty, and I have sent them far away, leaving their land in ruins"* (Isaiah 6:11-12).

Despite the warnings from several prophets, the Israelites were unable to avoid being taken into exile by two of the greatest superpowers of their day.

READ IT FOR YOURSELF

"THOSE OF YOU THAT SURVIVE WILL BE SCATTERED TO EVERY NATION ON EARTH, AND YOU WILL HAVE TO WORSHIP STONE AND WOOD IDOLS THAT NEVER HELPED YOU OR YOUR ANCESTORS. YOU WILL BE RESTLESS—ALWAYS LONGING FOR HOME, BUT NEVER ABLE TO RETURN. YOU WILL LIVE IN CONSTANT FEAR OF DEATH."

DEUTERONOMY 28:64–66

EZEKIEL

Ezekiel's prophetic activity spans one of the most important epochs in Jewish history. He served in Judah before and after King Nebuchadnezzar of Babylonia crushed Jerusalem, conquered the land and carried its inhabitants into exile. Ezekiel's messages came at a critical time when the international power structure was shifting.

Prior to the exile, Ezekiel warned his people of the judgment that would come if they lived in violation of God's law. After the exile, he spoke words of hope for their future—if only they would turn back to God.

Ezekiel is well-known for combining rather symbolic actions with his spoken messages. On one occasion, he lay on the ground for days at a time to symbolize the siege of Jerusalem. Later, he cut off his hair and saved only a few strands to represent the remnant of people who would survive God's judgment.

Perhaps Ezekiel's most famous vision was that of a valley full of dry bones that had life breathed into them once more. The bones reattached and the bodies were reconstituted. This startling vision illustrated the hope of a new life and a new future. God would bring his people back to life, no matter what they endured in Babylon.

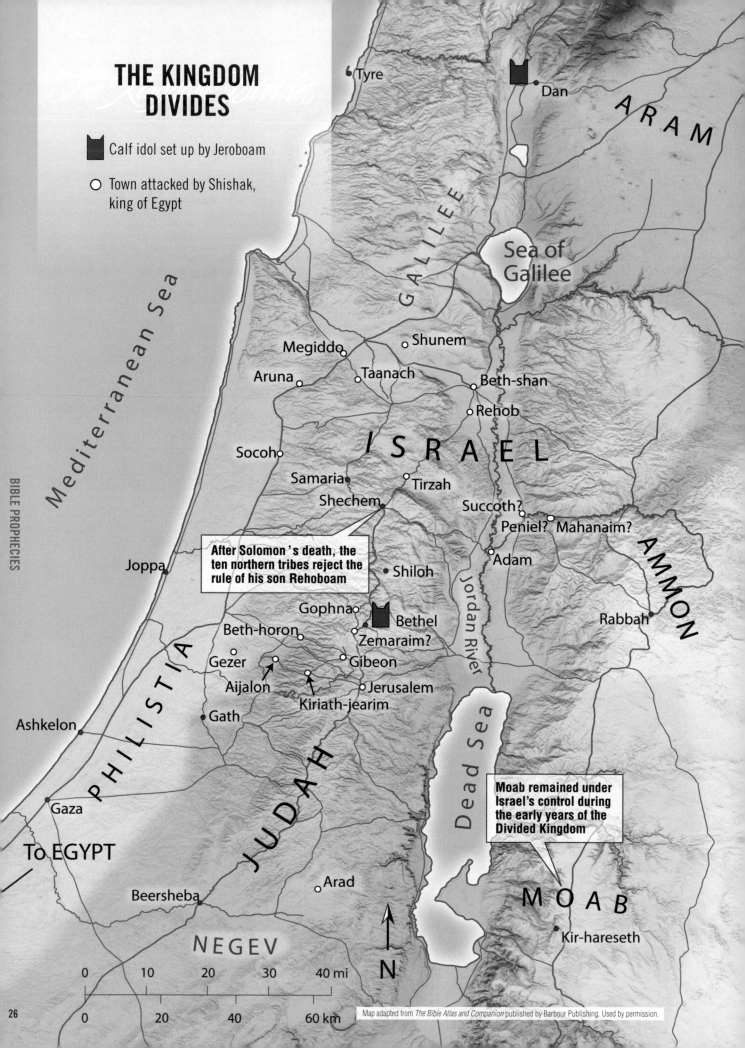

THE KINGDOM DIVIDES

■ Calf idol set up by Jeroboam

○ Town attacked by Shishak, king of Egypt

ARAM

Tyre

Dan

GALILEE

Sea of Galilee

Mediterranean Sea

Shunem

Megiddo

Aruna

Taanach

Beth-shan

Rehob

ISRAEL

Socoh

Samaria

Tirzah

Shechem

Succoth?

Peniel? Mahanaim?

AMMON

After Solomon's death, the ten northern tribes reject the rule of his son Rehoboam

Adam

Shiloh

Joppa

Gophna

Bethel

Rabbah

Beth-horon

Zemaraim?

Gezer

Gibeon

Jordan River

Aijalon

Kiriath-jearim

Jerusalem

PHILISTIA

Gath

Ashkelon

Dead Sea

Moab remained under Israel's control during the early years of the Divided Kingdom

JUDAH

Gaza

To EGYPT

Arad

M O A B

Beersheba

Kir-hareseth

NEGEV

| 0 | 10 | 20 | 30 | 40 mi |

| 0 | 20 | 40 | 60 km |

N

Map adapted from *The Bible Atlas and Companion* published by Barbour Publishing. Used by permission.

EVEN THOUGH THE LORD HAD COMMANDED THE ISRAELITES NOT TO WORSHIP

IDOLS, THEY DID IT ANYWAY. SO THE LORD MADE SURE THAT EVERY PROPHET

WARNED ISRAEL AND JUDAH WITH THESE WORDS: "I, THE LORD, COMMAND YOU

TO STOP DOING SINFUL THINGS AND START OBEYING MY LAWS AND TEACHINGS!

I GAVE THEM TO YOUR ANCESTORS, AND I TOLD MY SERVANTS THE PROPHETS TO

REPEAT THEM TO YOU." BUT THE ISRAELITES WOULD NOT LISTEN; THEY WERE

2 KINGS 17:12–15

AS STUBBORN AS THEIR ANCESTORS WHO HAD REFUSED TO WORSHIP THE LORD

THEIR GOD. THEY IGNORED THE LORD'S WARNINGS AND COMMANDS, AND THEY

REJECTED THE SOLEMN AGREEMENT HE HAD MADE WITH THEIR ANCESTORS.

THEY WORSHIPED WORTHLESS IDOLS AND BECAME WORTHLESS THEMSELVES.

THE LORD HAD TOLD THE ISRAELITES NOT TO DO THE THINGS THAT THE FOREIGN

NATIONS AROUND THEM WERE DOING, BUT ISRAEL BECAME JUST LIKE THEM.

AN ENDURING REMNANT

Saving a Few for a Great Purpose

READ IT FOR YOURSELF

"MY EYES HAVE SEEN WHAT A SINFUL NATION YOU ARE, AND I'LL WIPE YOU OUT. BUT I WILL LEAVE A FEW OF JACOB'S DESCENDANTS. I, THE LORD, HAVE SPOKEN!" AMOS 9:8

"THERE WERE AS MANY PEOPLE AS THERE ARE GRAINS OF SAND ALONG THE SEASHORE, BUT ONLY A FEW WILL SURVIVE TO COME BACK TO ISRAEL'S MIGHTY GOD." ISAIAH 10:21–22

War, invasion, and exile are just a few of the hardships documented in the historical books of the Old Testament. As we have seen, prophets claiming to have messages from God spoke of many of these events—or judgments, as they saw them. But the prophets also wrote about a remnant—a group of Israelites who would survive the exile and eventually return home.

The scribe Ezra, one such exile survivor, declared that *"for now, LORD God, you have shown great kindness to us. You made us truly happy by letting some of us settle in this sacred place and by helping us in our time of slavery"* (Ezra 9:8). The survivors Ezra referred to were those Israelites who returned from Babylonian captivity to help rebuild the temple in Jerusalem. The author of Ezra even included a detailed list of individuals who journeyed back to Jerusalem (Ezra 2), just as the ancient prophets had promised.

In a passage often associated with this event, the prophet Jeremiah said, *"I will bring the rest of my people home from the lands where I have scattered them, and they will grow into a mighty nation"* (Jeremiah 23:3; see also Jeremiah 30–33).

Some scholars believe that the prophet Isaiah also expressed his confidence in the divine preservation of a remnant by naming one of his sons Shearjashub, which in Hebrew means "a few will return" (see Isaiah 7:3).

Medieval map of Jerusalem

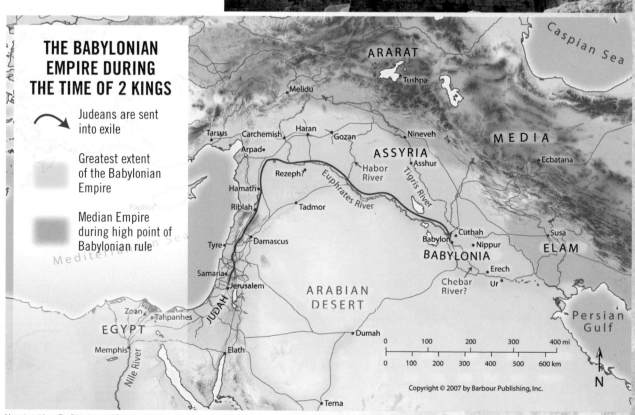

THE BABYLONIAN EMPIRE DURING THE TIME OF 2 KINGS

Judeans are sent into exile

Greatest extent of the Babylonian Empire

Median Empire during high point of Babylonian rule

ARARAT

Tushpa

Melidu

Tarsus
Carchemish
Haran
Gozan
Nineveh

MEDIA

Arpad
ASSYRIA
Asshur
Ecbatana

Rezeph?
Habor River

Hamath
Euphrates River
Tigris River

Riblah
Tadmor

Mediterranean Sea

Paphos

Tyre
Damascus

Babylon
Cuthah
Nippur
Susa

BABYLONIA
ELAM

Samaria

Jerusalem
Chebar River?
Erech
Ur

Zoan
Tahpanhes
JUDAH

ARABIAN DESERT

Persian Gulf

EGYPT

Dumah

Memphis
Nile River
Elath

| 0 | 100 | 200 | 300 | 400 mi |

| 0 | 100 | 200 | 300 | 400 | 500 | 600 km |

N

Tema

Copyright © 2007 by Barbour Publishing, Inc.

Map adapted from *The Bible Atlas and Companion* published by Barbour Publishing. Used by permission.

THE ISRAELITES RETURN HOME

The Rebuilding Begins

BIBLE PROPHECIES

The return from captivity of the surviving remnant of the Israelites fulfilled the hope of the prophets who spoke not just of judgment but also of restoration, reconciliation, and rebuilding.

This was Ezekiel's message from the Lord: *"But here is what I want you to tell the Israelites in Babylonia: It's true that I, the LORD God, have forced you out of your own country and made you live among foreign nations. But for now, I will be with you wherever you are, so that you can worship me. And someday, I will gather you from the nations where you are scattered and let you live in Israel again"* (Ezekiel 11:16–17).

The prophet Jeremiah also had a message of hope for the exiled people in Babylonia: *"After Babylonia has been the strongest nation for 70 years, I will be kind and bring you back to Jerusalem, just as I have promised. I will bless you with a future filled with hope—a future of success, not of suffering"* (Jeremiah 29:10–11).

According to Ezra's account of the return from exile, which took place around the year 539 BC, King Cyrus of Persia overthrew the Babylonian empire. At that time, Cyrus issued a decree that any of the Israelites who wanted to return home and help rebuild the temple in Jerusalem were free to do so (Ezra 1:1–3).

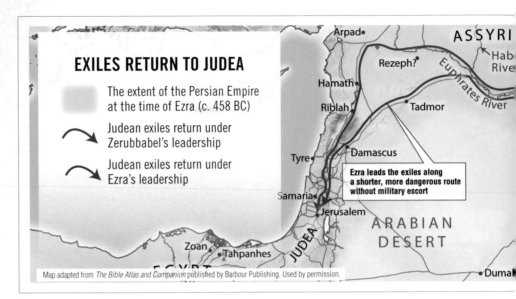

EXILES RETURN TO JUDEA

The extent of the Persian Empire at the time of Ezra (c. 458 BC)

Judean exiles return under Zerubbabel's leadership

Judean exiles return under Ezra's leadership

Ezra leads the exiles along a shorter, more dangerous route without military escort

Arpad • Rezeph? • Hamath • Riblah • Tadmor • Damascus • Tyre • Samaria • Jerusalem • Zoan • Tahpanhes • Dumah

ASSYRIA · Habor River · Euphrates River · ARABIAN DESERT · JUDEA · EGYPT

Map adapted from *The Bible Atlas and Companion* published by Barbour Publishing. Used by permission.

Some biblical interpreters believe that the words of the prophet Amos foretold the rebuilding of the temple: *"In the future, I will rebuild David's fallen kingdom. I will build it from its ruins and set it up again, just as it used to be"* (Amos 9:11). To the Israelites who returned to Jerusalem, the rebuilt temple symbolized their renewed relationship with God.

READ IT FOR YOURSELF

"THE LORD SAID: AT THAT TIME I WILL GATHER MY PEOPLE—THE LAME AND THE OUTCASTS, AND ALL OTHERS INTO WHOSE LIVES I HAVE BROUGHT SORROW. THEN THE LAME AND THE OUTCASTS WILL BELONG TO MY PEOPLE AND BECOME A STRONG NATION. I, THE LORD, WILL RULE THEM FROM MOUNT ZION FOREVER. MOUNT ZION IN JERUSALEM, GUARDIAN OF MY PEOPLE, YOU WILL RULE AGAIN."
MICAH 4:6–8

Cyrus restoring the vessels of the temple.

left: **Nehemiah Looks Upon the Ruins of Jerusalem**, c. 1896–1902
James Jacques Joseph Tissot

right: Israel despairing over the destruction of Jerusalem

Asshur

Ecbatana

's River

Cuthah

Babylon

Nippur

Susa

BABYLONIA

ELAM

Erech

Ur

Copyright © 2007
by Barbour Publishing, Inc.

Pe

READ IT FOR YOURSELF

"THE LORD ANSWERED,
'COULD A MOTHER FORGET
A CHILD WHO NURSES AT HER
BREAST? COULD SHE FAIL TO
LOVE AN INFANT WHO CAME
FROM HER OWN BODY? EVEN
IF A MOTHER COULD FORGET,
I WILL NEVER FORGET YOU.
A PICTURE OF YOUR CITY IS
DRAWN ON MY HAND. YOU ARE
ALWAYS IN MY THOUGHTS!
YOUR CITY WILL BE BUILT
FASTER THAN IT WAS
DESTROYED—THOSE WHO
ATTACKED IT WILL RETREAT
AND LEAVE.' "
ISAIAH 49:15–17

A miniature relief
carving of King
Cyrus of Persia.

PROPHECIES CONCERNING:
OTHER COUNTRIES

The Palaces of
Nimroud Restored
Thomas Mann Baynes

"WHEN THE KING OF NINEVEH HEARD WHAT WAS HAPPENING, HE ALSO DRESSED IN SACKCLOTH; HE LEFT THE ROYAL PALACE AND SAT IN DUST." JONAH 3:6

3

NATIONS IN CONFLICT

YOU CAN LEARN A LOT ABOUT A NATION BY THE ENEMIES IT MAKES.

The prophecies of the Old Testament concern not just the affairs of Israel but also those of its enemies—nations like Edom, Egypt, Assyria, and Babylonia. Some might wonder why a nation that claimed to be ruled by God would devote so many of its prayers and sacred writings to vengeance. Whatever the answer, it is important to understand the cultural background of these prophecies.

The Israelites descended from one family with twelve sons. This family remained a cohesive unit as it relocated from its home in Canaan (modern-day Palestine) to Egypt, where its descendants lived for centuries, clustered together in a region called Goshen. Over the years, what started as a family grew into a large nation.

This was a time when national survival depended on feudal alliances and military power. Inspired by a promise passed down by their ancestors, this family-turned-nation journeyed back to Canaan to reinhabit the land—a land that had been settled by others in the meantime. Under these circumstances, military strength and negotiating skills would prove essential.

Another key to understanding Israel's story is this: Israel was a nation whose religion was woven as tightly into its identity as were its politics. For much of its early history, Israel did not have separate governmental and religious structures. It functioned as a theocracy; the people perceived God to be their national leader.

For the Israelites, praying for their enemies' defeat and believing God would cast his strength their way in battle seemed reasonable and just. They clung to the hope that God would come through for them, that he would do what he had promised.

This is why the Old Testament prophets gave so much attention to Israel's allies and rivals. It's understandable that the hope of an army facing defeat or a political exile longing for home would at times come in the form of a prayer that God would bring vengeance on the opposition.

Though each of these prophecies concerns specific nations, and at times even specific cities, there is a larger issue addressed here. These judgments were not simply against Babylonia or Egypt or Tyre, but against any human enterprise that chooses to live cut off from God. Recognizing the dominant prophetic theme of these passages, we transform them from historical information into a compelling message for those seeking to live a life of faith today.

NINEVEH:
DREADED BY JONAH

Jonah thrown overboard to the whale.
Brill, Paul (1554–1626)

Reluctantly, Jonah journeyed to Nineveh in the end, and surprisingly, the city repented of its ways. But it was a short-lived contrition. In the seventh century BC, two ancient prophets, Nahum and Zephaniah, announced the eventual downfall of Assyria's capital. Their pronouncements came about a century after the Assyrian army defeated the northern kingdom of Israel and forced the people into exile.

Zephaniah foretold that Nineveh would become a desolate wilderness, good only for passing beasts, the object of rage and ridicule (Zephaniah 2:13–15). Nahum spoke of a destructive fire that would leave Nineveh unprotected, inflicting a fatal wound upon it (Nahum 3:13, 19).

continued on next page...

Nineveh, located in present-day Iraq, was the capital of Assyria, a nation that was notorious for its military aggression.

Nineveh figures prominently in the familiar story of Jonah, the reluctant prophet called by God to warn the Ninevites that they would be destroyed because of their evil ways. The basic details of Jonah's story are known to many—namely, his attempt to refuse God's call, resulting in an unpleasant man-overboard-swallowed-by-large-fish experience.

But less well-known is the reason for Jonah's reluctance: Nineveh was a dreaded enemy of Israel, Jonah's home country. What was asked of Jonah would be similar to asking a Jewish man in the 1940s to go and preach repentance to Germany under the Nazi regime.

Jonah didn't hesitate: He quickly ran the other way. Misguided though he was, it must have seemed the most natural response in the heat of the moment.

What became of Nineveh?

The city was conquered in 612 BC
by a coalition of Babylonians,
Medes, and Scythians. It was so
utterly destroyed that its location
was virtually forgotten. One
tradition claims that two hundred
years after Nineveh's fall, a great
army passed by without realizing
a great city had once stood there.
As for the general area, it ended up
serving shepherds who grazed their
sheep (the passing beasts), much as
Zephaniah said it would.

■ **SCRIPTURAL SOURCE**
I am Zephaniah, the son of Cushi,
the grandson of Gedaliah, the
great-grandson of Amariah, and the
great-great-grandson of Hezekiah.
When Josiah son of Amon was king
of Judah, the LORD gave me this
message . . .

The LORD will reach to the north
to crush Assyria
and overthrow Nineveh.
Herds of wild animals
will live in its rubble;
all kinds of desert owls
will perch on its stones
and hoot in the windows.
Noisy ravens will be heard
inside its buildings,
stripped bare of cedar.
This is the glorious city
that felt secure and said,
"I am the only one!"
Now it's merely ruins,
a home for wild animals.
Every passerby simply sneers
and makes vulgar signs.
ZEPHANIAH 1:1; 2:13–15

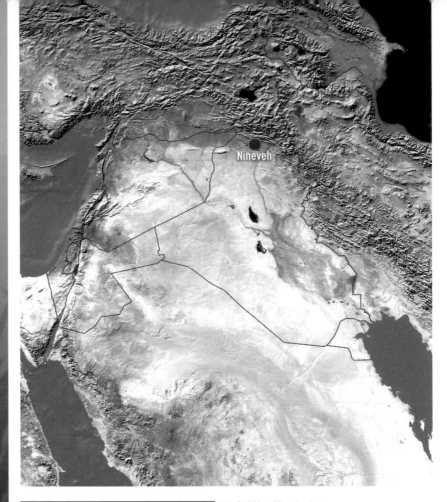

left: Relief from Nineveh, about
695 BC of a hunting scene.
Alabaster relief.
Pergamon
Museum

right: Assyrian warship 700–692 BC
From Nineveh

Nebi Yunus. Head of lamassu at the Iraqi
excavation of the entrance to a late Assyrian
building east of the mosque (1990).

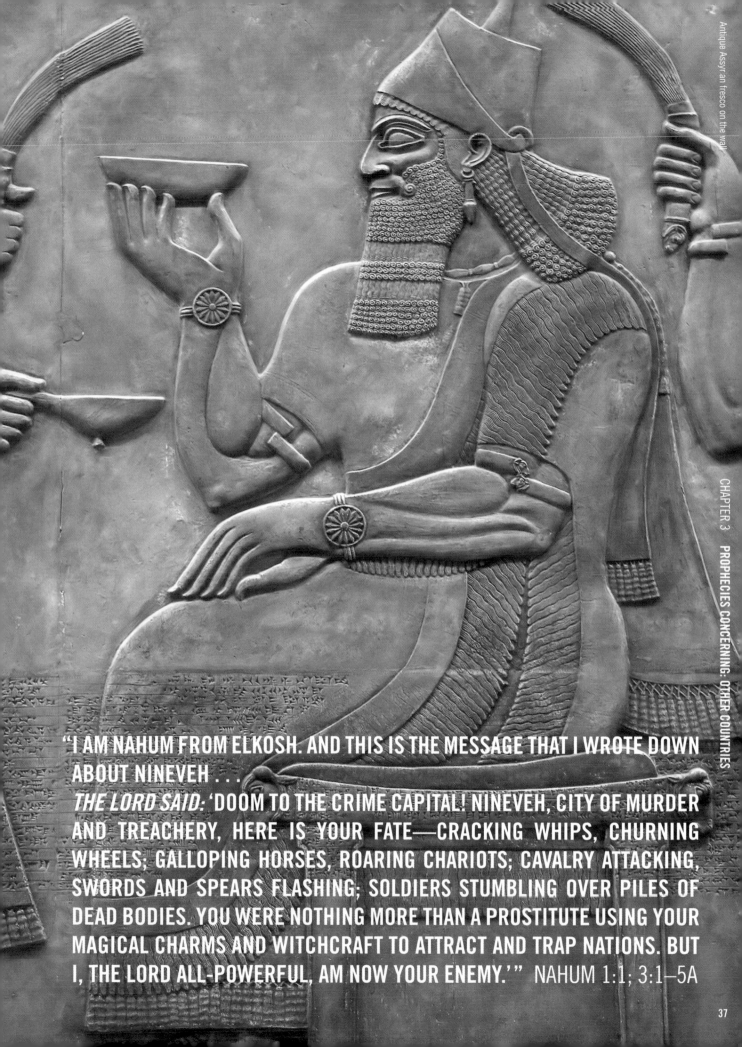

"I AM NAHUM FROM ELKOSH. AND THIS IS THE MESSAGE THAT I WROTE DOWN ABOUT NINEVEH . . .
THE LORD SAID: 'DOOM TO THE CRIME CAPITAL! NINEVEH, CITY OF MURDER AND TREACHERY, HERE IS YOUR FATE—CRACKING WHIPS, CHURNING WHEELS; GALLOPING HORSES, ROARING CHARIOTS; CAVALRY ATTACKING, SWORDS AND SPEARS FLASHING; SOLDIERS STUMBLING OVER PILES OF DEAD BODIES. YOU WERE NOTHING MORE THAN A PROSTITUTE USING YOUR MAGICAL CHARMS AND WITCHCRAFT TO ATTRACT AND TRAP NATIONS. BUT I, THE LORD ALL-POWERFUL, AM NOW YOUR ENEMY.'" NAHUM 1:1; 3:1—5A

JERICHO
AND THE CURSE

Joshua's battle against Jericho is one of the best-known (not to mention most unorthodox) military battles of the Bible. As the story goes, God himself devised the winning strategy: March around the city—once a day, every day for seven days—then six more times on the seventh day. Then: Everybody shout!

According to Joshua 6, the strategy brought Jericho's protective walls crashing down: What once had been a formidable fortress suddenly became a pile of stones—easy pickings.

Following Jericho's defeat, the Israelite commander, Joshua, announced a curse against anyone who might try to rebuild the city. According to Joshua's curse, that man's oldest son would die the moment he began laying the foundation, and the rest of his children would perish by the time the city gates were finished (Joshua 6:26).

A few centuries later, someone did rebuild Jericho. His unfortunate story is recorded in the book of 1 Kings:

While Ahab was king, a man from Bethel named Hiel rebuilt the town of Jericho. But while Hiel was laying the foundation for the town wall, his oldest son Abiram died. And while he was finishing the gates, his youngest son Segub died. This happened just as the LORD had told Joshua to say many years ago. (1 Kings 16:34)

ELIJAH

The prophecy concerning the rebuilding of Jericho was fulfilled in the 9th century BC during the time of the prophet Elijah. He lived during the reign of some of the most notorious tyrants ever seen in the northern kingdom of Israel—the reviled King Ahab and his Phoenician wife, Queen Jezebel. Jezebel's arrival was orchestrated in a trade agreement between Israel and Jezebel's father, the king of Tyre. With a new queen came a religion, Baal worship. This set the stage for Elijah's ministry and most of his conflicts he had with the ruling powers.

The accounts of Elijah (see 1 Kings 17–21) include a number of miracles. On one occasion, he predicted a three-year drought. During the worst of the drought, Elijah blessed a widow's dwindling supplies of flour and oil. Miraculously, they continued to provide for her family until the drought had ended. Elijah's prayers also brought that same widow's son back to life. Most spectacularly, the end of Elijah's life came not in the form of death, but as a chariot ride from earth to heaven.

above right: ***The Seven Trumpets of Jericho***
James Jacques Joseph Tissot

Jericho is believed to be one of the oldest cities in the world, dating back to 9000 BC. The Bible states that Jesus passed through Jericho, where he healed two blind men and converted a local tax collector named Zacharias. Christianity took hold in the city during the Byzantine era, and a church dedicated to Saint Eliseus was erected there.

Name Meaning	Moon
Founded	9000 BC
First Mentioned	Book of Numbers
Description	City of Palm Trees (Deuteronomy 34:3)

■ **SCRIPTURAL SOURCE**

On the seventh day, the army got up at daybreak. They marched slowly around Jericho the same as they had done for the past six days, except on this day they went around seven times. Then the priests blew the trumpets, and Joshua yelled: Get ready to shout! The Lord will let you capture this town. . . .

The priests blew their trumpets again, and the soldiers shouted as loud as they could. The walls of Jericho fell flat. Then the soldiers rushed up the hill, went straight into the town, and captured it. . . .

After Jericho was destroyed, Joshua warned the people, "Someday a man will rebuild Jericho, but the Lord will put a curse on him, and the man's oldest son will die when he starts to build the town wall. And by the time he finishes the wall and puts gates in it, all his children will be dead." The Lord helped Joshua in everything he did, and Joshua was famous everywhere in Canaan.

JOSHUA 6:15–16, 20, 26–27

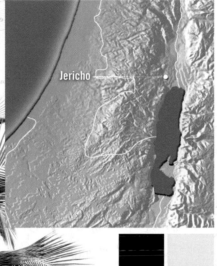

Jericho

IT IS INTERESTING TO NOTE THAT JERICHO, LOCATED ON THE WEST SIDE OF THE JORDAN RIVER, ABOUT TEN MILES NORTH OF THE DEAD SEA, IS ONE OF THE OLDEST CONTINUOUSLY INHABITED CITIES IN THE WORLD. IT HAD EXISTED AND THRIVED A LONG TIME BEFORE JOSHUA'S ROUNDABOUT ATTACK.

RAHAB

The prostitute Rahab assisted the Israelite spies before the invasion of Jericho. She and her family were spared from death, and they were allowed to live among the Israelites. Rahab is listed in Matthew's genealogy as an ancestor of both Jesus and King David (Matthew 1:1–18).

BABYLONIA
THE GREAT FALL

By the time that Babylonia had become a regional superpower and a growing threat to peace in the ancient Middle East, Israel had divided into the northern and southern kingdoms. Assyria, to the east, eventually conquered the northern kingdom (referred to as Israel). But it was Babylonia to the south (in what is southeastern Iraq today) that threatened the southern kingdom of Judah, all that remained of the once unified nation of Israel.

It was Babylonia, under Nebuchad-nezzar, that finally captured Jerusalem, Judah's capital, and carried its people into exile. It was Babylon, the kingdom's capital, that served as the backdrop to the story of Daniel, a young exile who was among those taken from Jerusalem to be incorporated into the conquering culture, as was the custom of the day (Daniel 1). It was Babylonia that played a starring role in the ancient prophecies of men like Isaiah, Ezekiel, and Jeremiah.

The prophet Isaiah lived in Judah at a time when Babylonia's military threat was escalating. Around 710 BC, he predicted three things: that the Medes (from what is now northeastern Iran) would rise against Babylon, that Babylon would be destroyed just as sure as the cities of Sodom and Gomorrah had been centuries before,

and that it would never be settled again, not even by wandering shepherds (Isaiah 13:17–22).

What happened?

Babylon was indeed captured by the Medes in 539 BC. It was completely ruined by the first century. Today, it is home to wild animals; it is mostly uninhabited except for traveling tourists or archaeologists. The city is described as a heap of rubble.

■ SCRIPTURAL SOURCE

I, the LORD, am sending
a wind to destroy
the people of Babylonia
and Babylon, its capital.
Foreign soldiers will come
from every direction,
and when the disaster is over,
Babylonia will be empty
and worthless. . . .
My people, I am on your side,
and I will take revenge
on Babylon.
I will cut off its water supply,
and its stream will dry up.
Babylon will be a pile of rubble
where only jackals live,
and everyone will be afraid
to walk among the ruins.
JEREMIAH 51:1–2, 36–37

Detail of the Ishtar Gate

Babylonia
(around 600 BC)

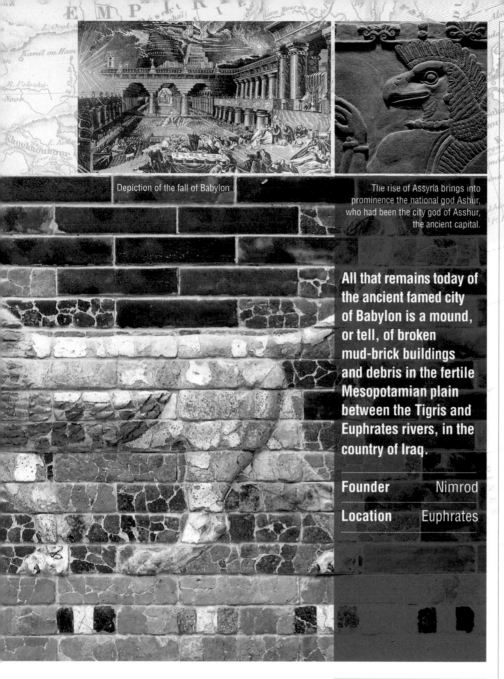

Depiction of the fall of Babylon

The rise of Assyria brings into prominence the national god Ashur, who had been the city god of Asshur, the ancient capital.

All that remains today of the ancient famed city of Babylon is a mound, or tell, of broken mud-brick buildings and debris in the fertile Mesopotamian plain between the Tigris and Euphrates rivers, in the country of Iraq.

Founder	Nimrod
Location	Euphrates

"BABYLON, BE SILENT! SIT IN THE DARK. NO LONGER WILL NATIONS ACCEPT YOU AS THEIR QUEEN. I WAS ANGRY WITH MY PEOPLE. SO I LET YOU TAKE THEIR LAND AND BRING DISGRACE ON THEM. YOU SHOWED THEM NO MERCY, BUT WERE ESPECIALLY CRUEL TO THOSE WHO WERE OLD. YOU THOUGHT THAT YOU WOULD BE QUEEN FOREVER. YOU DIDN'T CARE WHAT YOU DID; IT NEVER ENTERED YOUR MIND THAT YOU MIGHT GET CAUGHT." ISAIAH 47:5–7

POINT OF INTEREST

Considered one of the original Seven Wonders of the World, The Hanging Gardens were built by Nebuchadnezzar II around 600 BC near present-day Al Hillah in Iraq (formerly Babylon). He built the gardens as a consolation to his wife, who missed the natural surroundings of her homeland in Persia.

JEREMIAH

Jeremiah prophesied to the people of Judah just before the fall of the nation and the

capture of Jerusalem, its capital city.

After Nebuchadnezzar, king of Babylonia, captured Jerusalem, the conquering army deported many of the people into exile. Though the city was almost completely destroyed, Jeremiah returned and lived in its battered remains. According to tradition, it was there that he wrote the Old Testament book of Lamentations, a collection of funeral dirges mourning Judah's fate.

Jeremiah's prophecies were not well received, however. According to one tradition, he was stoned to death by his own people; evidently they had grown tired of hearing his condemnations of their idolatry. The Bible, however, presents Jeremiah as someone who remained true to what he saw as his calling, no matter what the consequences.

EGYPT
A WEAKENED EMPIRE

Egypt looms large in Israel's history. As a neighbor to the southwest on the fertile banks of the Nile River, Egypt often played a role in the development of Israel. Abraham and his grandson Jacob both took refuge in Egypt during times of famine. Joseph, one of Jacob's sons, was even appointed by the king of Egypt to serve as a governor. It was also in Egypt that Jacob's descendants grew into the nation of Israel, and from Egypt that they fled in the Exodus. Centuries later, Jesus, Mary, and Joseph escaped the murderous Herod by finding refuge in Egypt.

Egypt was a world power from 4300 BC until about 600 BC—sometimes wielding its might over Israel and sometimes serving as a refuge for exiles. Nevertheless, the prophets Ezekiel and Jeremiah spoke of Egypt's eventual fall from power (Jeremiah 46; Ezekiel 29–32). Ezekiel wrote that Egypt would recover from desolation (perhaps a reference to an attack by the Babylonians), but that it would never again rule as widely (Ezekiel 29:13–15).

History shows that Egypt faced many defeats, yet with each one it reestablished itself as a nation. Ezekiel's prophecy seems to have been fulfilled in that Egypt no longer reached beyond its own borders the way it had in the past.

Egypt

POINT OF INTEREST

In the 26th century BC three kings ordered the construction of three huge pyramids that would be their tombs. The kings were Khufu, his son Khafre, and his grandson Menkure. The first of these three pyramids is known as the Great Pyramid. It was the largest pyramid ever built.

Egypt is famous for its ancient civilization and some of the world's most well-known monuments including the Giza pyramid complex and its Great Sphinx. The southern city of Luxor contains numerous ancient artifacts such as the Karnak Temple and the Valley of the Kings. Egypt is widely regarded as an important political and cultural nation of the Middle East.

Capital	Cairo
Language	Arabic
Today's Ethnic Groups	98% Egyptian
	1% Nubian
	1% Greek
First Dynasty	c. 3150 BC

The city of Cairo

EZEKIEL 29:1-16

TEN YEARS AFTER KING JEHOIACHIN

and the rest of us had been led away as prisoners to Babylonia, the LORD spoke to me on the twelfth day of the tenth month. He said: Ezekiel, son of man, condemn the king of Egypt. Tell him and his people that I am saying: King of Egypt, you were like a giant crocodile lying in a river. You acted as though you owned the Nile and made it for yourself. But now I, the LORD God, am your enemy! I will put a hook in your jaw and pull you out of the water, and all the fish in your river will stick to your scaly body. I'll throw you and the fish into the desert, and your body will fall on the hard ground. You will be left unburied, and wild animals and birds will eat your flesh. Then everyone in Egypt will know that I am the LORD. You and your nation refused to help the people of Israel and were nothing more than a broken stick. When they reached out to you for support, you broke in half, cutting their arms and making them fall. So I, the LORD God, will send troops to attack you, king of Egypt. They will kill your people and livestock, until your land is a barren desert. Then you will know that I have done these things.

You claimed that you made the Nile River and control it. Now I am turning against you and your river. Your nation will be nothing but an empty wasteland all the way from the town of Migdol in the north to Aswan in the south, and as far as the border of Ethiopia. No human or animal will even dare travel through Egypt, because no sign of life will be found there for 40 years. It will be the most barren place on earth. Every city in Egypt will lie in ruins during those 40 years, and I will scatter your people throughout the nations of the world. Then after those 40 years have passed, I will bring your people back from the places where I scattered them. They will once again live in their homeland in southern Egypt. But they will be a weak kingdom and won't ever be strong enough to rule nations, as they did in the past. My own people Israel will never again depend on your nation. In fact, when the Israelites remember what happened to you Egyptians, they will realize how wrong they were to turn to you for help. Then the Israelites will know that I, the LORD God, did these things.

A PROMISED

THE RAZING OF TYRE

As far as cities go, Tyre had it all—vast wealth built on lucrative trade with its neighbors, not to mention natural defenses that were the envy of the region.

Tyre was a Phoenician city-state on the Mediterranean coast. It existed in two parts: an older port on the mainland and an island city about a half a mile from the coast. Most of the population lived on the island, and those who lived on the mainland would flee there during times of invasion.

Tyre is first mentioned in the Bible as part of the inheritance belonging to an Israelite tribe called Asher. Though Asher never incorporated Tyre into its holdings, the two developed a strong commercial alliance, trading wood, building materials, and labor for crops and livestock.

By the time Isaiah, Jeremiah, and Ezekiel were prophesying, however, Tyre was no longer considered an ally. The three prophets accused Tyre of exploiting its neighbors politically, pitting one against the other, trading unscrupulously, and engaging in idolatry and immorality. At this time, speaking against a city as prosperous as Tyre and warning of its destruction would have seemed absurd. Yet, this is exactly what Isaiah, Jeremiah, and Ezekiel did.

Around 315 BC, their warnings of doom came true: The Macedonian conqueror Alexander the Great destroyed Tyre. Using massive quantities of stone, timber, and dirt from the mainland, Alexander built a causeway to the island. The seemingly impregnable city stood no chance. This scene was reminiscent of Ezekiel's prophecy (see Ezekiel 26:12). No longer a symbol of success, the ruins of Tyre serve mostly as a tourist destination today.

A few centuries later, Jesus referred to Tyre in an unflattering light, comparing its people to the Galilean towns that rejected him outright (Matthew 11:21). It was in Tyre that he met the Syrophoenician woman and healed her daughter (Mark 7:24–30).

■ **SCRIPTURAL SOURCE:** *The troops will steal your valuable possessions; they will break down your walls, and crush your expensive houses. Then the stones and wood and all the remains will be dumped into the sea. You will have no reason to sing or play music on harps, because I will turn you into a bare rock where fishermen can dry their nets. And you will never rebuild your city. I, the LORD God, make this promise.* EZEKIEL 26:12–14

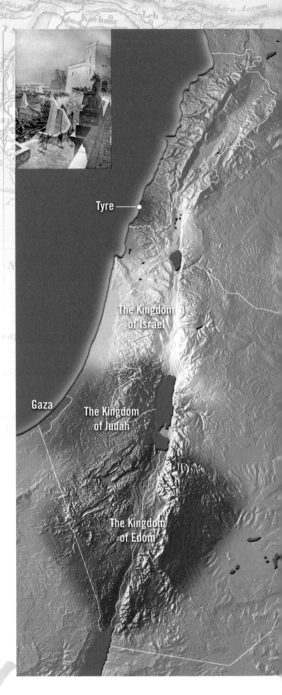

VENGEANCE ON EDOM

A deep animosity existed between Judah (the southern kingdom of Israel) and Edom, its neighbor to the south.

The two nations had descended from twin brothers, Jacob and Esau. According to Genesis, the two brothers vied for the leadership and birthright of their family.

Jacob's side of the family tree can be described as follows: Jacob's name was changed to Israel, thus his descendants were called Israelites.

VENGEANCE

Following the death of King Solomon around 922 BC, the ten northern tribes rebelled against Solomon's successor (his son, Rehoboam) and formed the kingdom of Israel; the two southern tribes became known as the kingdom of Judah, located west of the Dead Sea.

Esau was also known as Edom, thus his descendants were known as the Edomites.

Just as the twin brothers lived in conflict, their descendants seem to have held onto old grudges. When the Israelites traveled from Egypt to Canaan, they tried to cross Edom's territory, but they were denied passage (Numbers 20:14–21). During the following centuries, Edom served as Israel's rival when the latter resettled in Canaan. Sometimes the two countries traded with each other, and on a few occasions they even formed a military alliance. In the end, though, when the Babylonians attacked Jerusalem, Judah's capital, the Edomites took advantage of the situation, occupying territory that had belonged to Judah.

Given the history between the two nations, several Israelite prophets— including Isaiah, Ezekiel, Joel, Amos, Obadiah, and Malachi—spoke unfavorably of Edom. They claimed the land of Esau's descendants would become a barren wasteland.

By the sixth century BC, Edom was indeed in decline. Today, no living tribe or people claims descent from the Edomites. Some mistakenly believe Arabs to be descendants of Edom,

but even in the days of ancient Israel, Arabs were already differentiated from the Edomites. (Compare the mention of Edom in 2 Chronicles 8:17 and the mention of Arabia in 2 Chronicles 9:14.)

The prophet Obadiah compared Israel to a fire and Edom to straw (Obadiah 18). While the Edomites wielded power at one time, today others inhabit their land.

■ **SCRIPTURAL SOURCE:** *The LORD God then said, "The people of Edom are guilty of taking revenge on Judah. So I will punish Edom by killing all its people and livestock. It will be an empty wasteland all the way from Teman to Dedan. I will send my own people to take revenge on the Edomites by making them feel my fierce anger. And when I punish them, they will know that I am the LORD God."* EZEKIEL 25:12–14

DESOLATE GAZA

Gaza is an agriculturally rich land just three miles from the Mediterranean Sea, southwest of Judah.

It is first mentioned in the Bible as a boundary marker for the land of the Canaanites: from Sidon in the north to Gaza in the south. When Israel set out to reinhabit Canaan, Gaza was included in the tribe of Judah's territory (Joshua 15:47). Today, the city sits at the heart of the conflict over territory controlled by Israel and populated by Palestinians.

Gaza was one of five key Philistine cities collectively known as the Pentapolis (Joshua 13:3). The other four cities were Ashdod, Ashkelon, Gath, and Ekron. Ancient Gaza is perhaps best known for its role in Samson's story. In one of the strong man's touted feats, he carried off the doors and posts of Gaza's city gate. After Samson was captured and blinded, he was imprisoned in Gaza. There he performed his final act, destroying the temple of Dagon and dying amid the rubble (Judges 16:21–30).

Prophets like Amos, Jeremiah, Zephaniah, and Zechariah issued dire warnings against Gaza and the other cities of the Pentapolis. Such warnings served to convey the extent of God's punishment for those who refused to obey him.

■ **SCRIPTURAL SOURCE:** *The LORD said: "I will punish Philistia for countless crimes, and I won't change my mind. They dragged off my people from town after town to sell them as slaves to the Edomites. That's why I will burn down the walls and fortresses of the city of Gaza."* AMOS 1:6–7

ALEXANDER THE GREAT
A GOAT FROM THE WEST

BIBLE PROPHECIES

Alexander the Great assumed command of the Macedonian army when he was just twenty years old. Before dying suddenly at the age of thirty-three, he conquered a vast region stretching from Greece to India. His far-reaching control has left a mark on cultures around the world to this very day. After his death, Alexander's territory was divided among four generals.

The prophet Daniel lived 250 years before Alexander, yet many regard his prophecy about a "goat from the west" as an unmistakable description of the mighty conqueror.

"THEN A MIGHTY KING WILL COME TO POWER AND WILL BE ABLE TO DO WHATEVER HE PLEASES. BUT SUDDENLY HIS KINGDOM WILL BE CRUSHED AND SCATTERED TO THE FOUR CORNERS OF THE EARTH, WHERE FOUR MORE KINGDOMS WILL RISE. BUT THESE WON'T BE RULED BY HIS DESCENDANTS OR BE AS POWERFUL AS HIS KINGDOM." DANIEL 11:3–4

Marble head of Alexander the Great

THE EMPIRE OF ALEXANDER
334-323 B.C.
→ Conquest course of Alexander
✕ Battle
◯ Siege
● Town founded by Alexander
● Settlement of existing town
≍ Mountain pass
= Greek colony
······· Persian royal road
A. Alexandria

0   500 km

■ SCRIPTURAL SOURCE

Daniel wrote:

In the third year of King Belshazzar of Babylonia, I had a second vision in which I was in Susa, the chief city of Babylonia's Elam Province. I was beside the Ulai River, when I looked up and saw a ram standing there with two horns on its head—both of them were long, but the second one was longer than the first. The ram went charging toward the west, the north, and the south. No other animals were strong enough to oppose him, and nothing could save them from his power. So he did as he pleased and became even more powerful. I kept on watching and saw a goat come from the west and charge across the entire earth, without even touching the ground. Between his eyes was a powerful horn, and with tremendous anger the goat started toward the ram that I had seen beside the river. The goat was so fierce that its attack broke both horns of the ram, leaving him powerless. Then the goat stomped on the ram, and no one could do anything to help. After this, the goat became even more powerful. But at the peak of his power, his mighty horn was broken, and four other mighty horns took its place—one pointing to the north and one to the east, one to the south and one to the west.

Daniel 8:1–8

above: Detail of the Alexander Mosaic, representing Alexander the Great on his horse Bucephalus.

left: 15th century Persian miniature painting from Herat depicting Iskander, the Persian name for Alexander the Great, who was venerated by Muslims as Dhul-Qarnayn

Alexander the Great was one of the most successful military commanders of all time and is presumed undefeated in battle. By the time of his death, he had conquered most of the world known to the ancient Greeks.

Reign	336–323 BC
Born	July 20, 356 BC
Birthplace	Pella, Macedonia
Died	June 10 or June 11, 323 BC (aged 32)
Place of death	Babylon
Successor	Alexander IV

POINT OF INTEREST

Persepolis was the capital of the Persian Empire. Alexander described it to the Macedonians as their worst enemy among the cities of Asia, and he gave it over to the soldiers to plunder, with the exception of the royal palace.

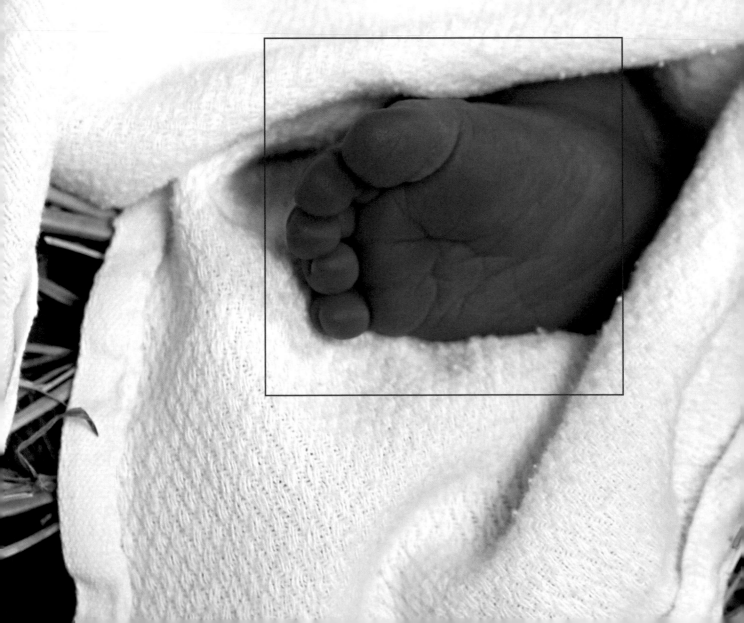

PROPHECIES CONCERNING:

THE BIRTH OF JESUS

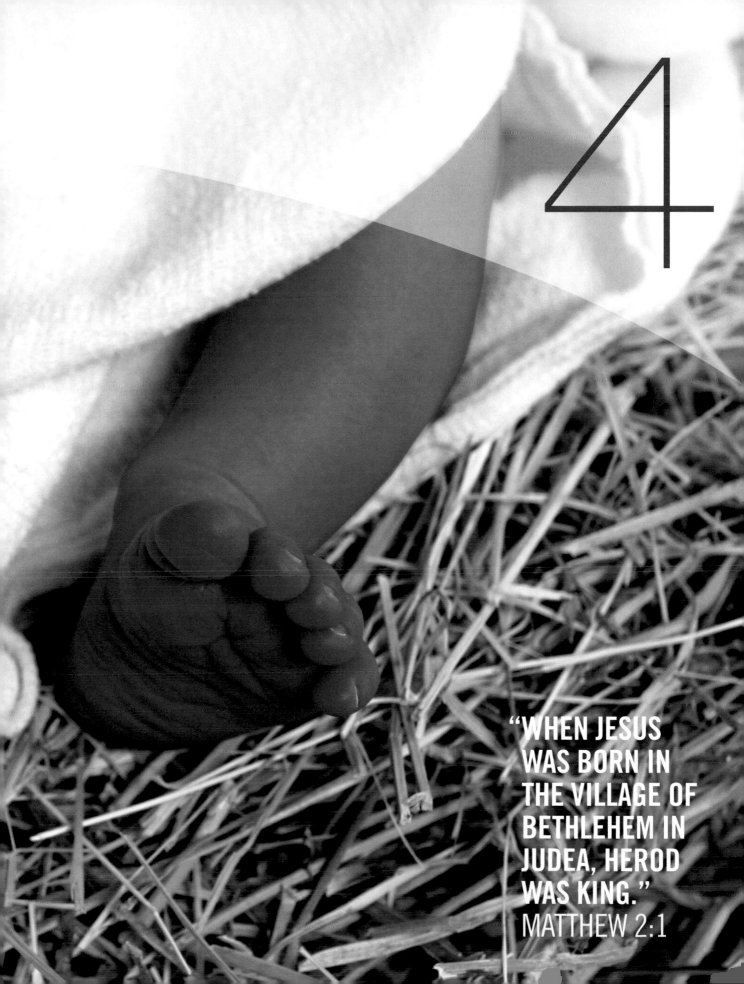

4

"WHEN JESUS WAS BORN IN THE VILLAGE OF BETHLEHEM IN JUDEA, HEROD WAS KING."
MATTHEW 2:1

THE HOPE OF THE OLD TESTAMENT HUNG ON A PROMISE WHISPERED BY ANCIENT PROPHETS: SOMEDAY A DELIVERER—A MESSIAH—WOULD APPEAR, TO RESCUE HUMANITY FROM SIN AND DESPAIR.

Sometimes prophets spoke in language so cryptic that the full impact of their words would only be discovered centuries later. Other prophecies described the Messiah's advent in surprising detail—who he would be, where he would be born, and what circumstances would surround his birth.

The authors of the four New Testament Gospels—books that tell the good news of Jesus Christ and which are the primary source of biographical information about him—note the many connections between the prophets of old and the first-century world in which Jesus lived and taught. Matthew, in particular, often referred to the prophets of the Old Testament. His first readers were Jewish and would have been well acquainted with the prophetic tradition that receives such strong emphasis in Matthew's Gospel.

Whether directly quoting the prophets or simply alluding to them, the Gospel writers saw their predecessors' words as confirmation that Jesus was, in fact, the Messiah that Israel had been waiting for.

ANNA

The prophets of the Bible include some surprising characters, like an 84-year-old widow named Anna, who prophesied a few days after Jesus' birth. Luke's Gospel tells her story in just a few sentences. Anna had been married for just seven years when her husband died. Apparently, she remained single the rest of her life, serving God in the temple, praying, and fasting. Luke says she was at the temple "night and day."

On the day the infant Jesus was brought to the temple to be presented—as was the custom then—a man named Simeon recognized Jesus as the fulfillment of God's promise to send someone to save his people (see Luke 2:29–32).

Upon hearing Simeon's proclamation, Anna began to spread the word about Jesus to those who "hoped for Jerusalem to be set free" (Luke 2:36–38).

IT'S ALL IN THE DETAILS

The Beginning of the Jewish People

The Bible's first promise of a Messiah was the direct result of Adam and Eve's fall into sin. After a snake convinced humankind's first couple to disobey God's command, he revealed that a descendant of Eve would be sent to deal with the snake once and for all (Genesis 3:15). Christian tradition has long understood this to be the earliest reference to a Messiah who would fight back against the oppressive power of sin, as personified by the snake.

Later, the Old Testament prophet Isaiah foretold that a virgin would become miraculously pregnant and give birth to a son (Isaiah 7:14)—not just any son, but a son named Immanuel, or "God is with us." Two Gospel writers identified Mary, the mother of Jesus, as the ultimate fulfillment of this prophecy (Matthew 1:18–23; Luke 1:26–38).

Yet another Old Testament prophet, Micah, foretold that Israel's Savior would come from the obscure town of Bethlehem (located about six miles south of Jerusalem). He would descend, according to Micah, from the tribe of Judah, one of twelve family lines comprising the nation of Israel. This individual would rule and bring peace to the nation (Micah 5:2–5). Centuries later, Matthew quoted the prophet Micah, declaring to his readers that Jesus had fulfilled this prophecy (Matthew 2:1, 5–6).

These three prophecies, among others, were indications of the way God's promise to bring salvation to the world would be fulfilled, offering ordinary people in the future opportunities to identify the Messiah they'd been waiting for.

READ IT FOR YOURSELF

"ONE MONTH LATER GOD SENT THE ANGEL GABRIEL TO THE TOWN OF NAZARETH IN GALILEE WITH A MESSAGE FOR A VIRGIN NAMED MARY. SHE WAS ENGAGED TO JOSEPH FROM THE FAMILY OF KING DAVID." LUKE 1:26–27

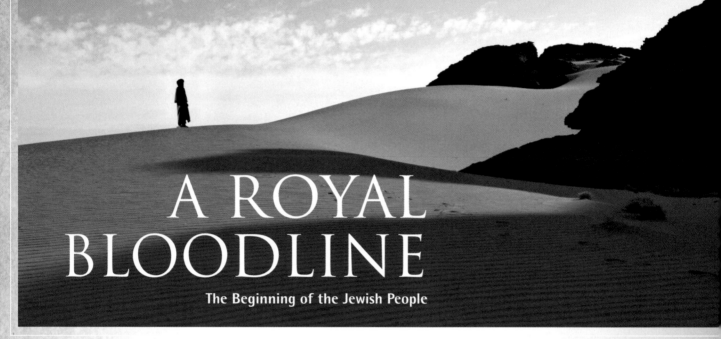

> "THE LORD SAID TO ABRAM: LEAVE YOUR COUNTRY, YOUR FAMILY, AND YOUR RELATIVES AND GO TO THE LAND THAT I WILL SHOW YOU. I WILL BLESS YOU AND MAKE YOUR DESCENDANTS INTO A GREAT NATION. YOU WILL BECOME FAMOUS AND BE A BLESSING TO OTHERS."
>
> GENESIS 12:1–3

A ROYAL BLOODLINE

The Beginning of the Jewish People

ABRAHAM

While the Israelites waited for a Messiah to deliver them, they clung with hope to the promises God had made to their ancestors long ago.

God promised the elderly Abraham, the great patriarch of the Israelites, that he would father many nations and that God would bless the entire world through his descendants (Genesis 12:1–3; 22:16–18).

Just two generations later, God repeated himself to Abraham's grandson Jacob: *"Your descendants will spread over the earth in all directions and will become as numerous as the specks of dust. Your family will be a blessing to all people"* (Genesis 28:14).

It was the apostle Paul , whose theologically insightful letters would one day be included in the New Testament, who connected Jesus to God's ancient covenant with Abraham. *"That is how it is with the promises God made to Abraham and his descendant,"* wrote Paul in his letter to the Galatians. *"The promises were not made to many descendants, but only to one, and that one is Christ"* (Galatians 3:16). Paul recognized Jesus as a descendant of Abraham—and therefore, as the fulfillment of God's promise of salvation to Abraham, his descendants, and the world.

KING DAVID

The story of Israel's greatest king, David, reveals yet another indication of the coming of the promised Messiah.

While God promised to bless Abraham, his covenant with David promised the king that his royal dynasty would never end. God said to David, *"I will make sure that one of your descendants will always be king"* (2 Samuel 7:16; see also Psalms 89:3–4; 132:11; Isaiah 11:1; Jeremiah 23:5).

Because God promised David a never-ending dynasty, the prophets deduced that the ultimate heir to David's throne must be the Messiah. Isaiah, for example, made a statement that, in Christian tradition, connects David's bloodline with the future Messiah: *"A child has been born for us. We have been given a son who will be our ruler. His names will be Wonderful Advisor and Mighty God, Eternal Father and Prince of Peace. His power will never end; peace will last forever. He will rule David's kingdom and make it grow strong. He will always rule with honesty and justice. The LORD All-Powerful will make certain that all of this is done"* (Isaiah 9:6–7).

The Israelites expected their Messiah to be both a descendant of Abraham and heir to David's throne. It's no surprise, then, that Matthew and Luke include genealogies confirming his bloodline, in their accounts of his life (Matthew 1:1–17; Luke 3:23–38). This was their way of demonstrating to their readers that Jesus was indeed the promised Messiah foretold by the Old Testament prophets. Luke's genealogy concludes by designating Jesus as the Son of God.

READ IT FOR YOURSELF

"YOU SAID, 'DAVID, MY SERVANT, IS MY CHOSEN ONE, AND THIS IS THE AGREEMENT I MADE WITH HIM: DAVID, ONE OF YOUR DESCENDANTS WILL ALWAYS BE KING.'"
PSALM 89:3–4

"Jesus Christ came from the family of King David and also from the family of Abraham.... There were 14 generations from Abraham to David. There were also 14 from David to the exile in Babylonia and 14 more to the birth of the Messiah."
MATTHEW 1:1A, 17

SURVIVAL OF A KING

"IN RAMAH A VOICE IS HEARD, CRYING AND WEEPING LOUDLY. RACHEL MOURNS FOR HER CHILDREN AND REFUSES TO BE COMFORTED, BECAUSE THEY ARE DEAD." JEREMIAH 31:15

The Israelites had been promised a Messiah born of the line of King David. But by the time Jesus was born, the Jewish people were under the thumb of a very different kind of king.

Herod the Great ruled Palestine from 37 BC to 4 BC. His territory included Bethlehem, the place of Jesus' birth. But Herod was not the rightful heir to David's throne: he was a mere client king. He served at the pleasure of the Roman Empire, which controlled the Mediterranean world at the time.

Herod was famous for his massive building projects, like the temple in Jerusalem. He was also known for his cruelty and paranoia. When magi—astronomers from the East—arrived in search of the recently born "king of the Jews," Herod sensed a threat to his throne (Matthew 2:1–2). He knew that most Jews wanted to escape from Roman rule, and he worried that they were devising a plan to overthrow him.

Herod was also aware of the old prophecies about a Messiah who would come to save his people. According to Matthew, *"Herod brought together the chief priests and the teachers of the Law of Moses and asked them, 'Where will the Messiah be born?' "* (Matthew 2:4). Their answer? Bethlehem of Judea, just as the prophet Micah had said.

Herod was not one to give up his throne willingly. He told the magi to go and find the baby, then return with the location of the child so he, too, could go and "worship." When the magi did not return, Herod

ordered the killing of *"all the boys who lived in or near Bethlehem and were two years old and younger"* (Matthew 2:16). Hearing of this dreadful decree, Joseph and Mary took their infant son Jesus and quickly fled to Egypt for protection.

In telling this story, Matthew quotes two Old Testament prophecies, connecting them to Herod's killing of innocent children and Jesus' escape. The first is a prophecy that God will call his "son out of Egypt" (Matthew 2:15). The prophet Hosea wrote these words centuries earlier, referring most immediately to the nation of Israel and the Exodus, when Moses led his people out of slavery in Egypt (Hosea 11:1). Matthew applied these words to Jesus, the Messiah who returned from Egypt after Herod's death.

Matthew also quoted the prophet Jeremiah's vivid description of Rachel, the wife of Jacob, Abraham's grandson, as she mourned and wept for her children. In Jeremiah's original prophecy, Rachel represented all the Israelites, who were also in mourning, just before their restoration from exile. For Matthew, Rachel represented all the Jewish

mothers in Bethlehem who were lamenting the fate of their slaughtered children. Despite the pain many suffered because of Herod's cruelty, the fact that the young Messiah survived brought hope for those grieving families.

READ IT FOR YOURSELF

"WHEN ISRAEL WAS A CHILD, I LOVED HIM, AND I CALLED MY SON OUT OF EGYPT." HOSEA 11:1

IMMANUEL, GOD IS WITH US

A Virgin Would Become Pregnant and Bear a Son Named Immanuel

One short sentence from the book of Isaiah (mentioned earlier in this chapter) contains two earth-shattering prophecies identifying the coming Messiah: *"A virgin is pregnant; she will have a son and will name him Immanuel"* (Isaiah 7:14).

The original setting for this prophecy was the court of Ahaz, king of Judah. God invited Ahaz to request a sign of his protection, but Ahaz stubbornly refused. God decided to give Ahaz a sign anyway—a virgin would become pregnant and bear a son named Immanuel. This sign and the accompanying promise of Israel's rescue were meant to be an encouragement to Ahaz, who was fighting against fierce enemies at the time, that he and his people would ultimately prevail.

But according to Mathew, Isaiah's prophecy saw its ultimate fulfillment in the birth of Jesus to the virgin Mary. In Matthew's own words, *"The Lord's promise came true, just as the prophet had said, 'A virgin will have a baby boy, and he will be called Immanuel,' which means 'God is with us'"* (Matthew 1:22–23).

The name "God is with us" signifies more than just God's protection. It refers to God's literal, tangible presence on earth. This was the promise the prophets dreamed about—a promise that was fulfilled by Jesus (John 1:14).

> **"THE WORD BECAME A HUMAN BEING AND LIVED HERE WITH US. WE SAW HIS TRUE GLORY, THE GLORY OF THE ONLY SON OF THE FATHER. FROM HIM THE COMPLETE GIFTS OF UNDESERVED GRACE AND TRUTH HAVE COME DOWN TO US."** JOHN 1:14

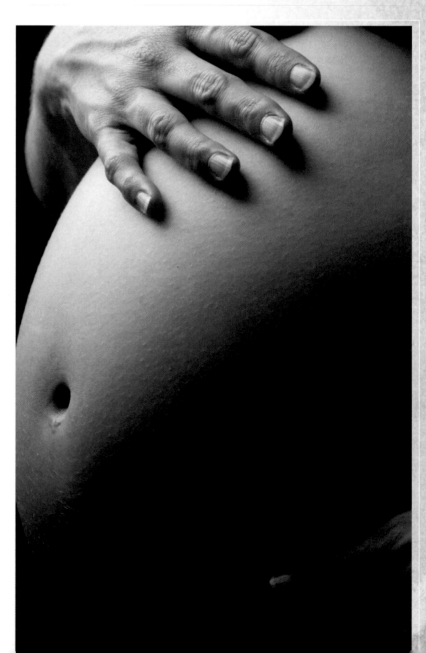

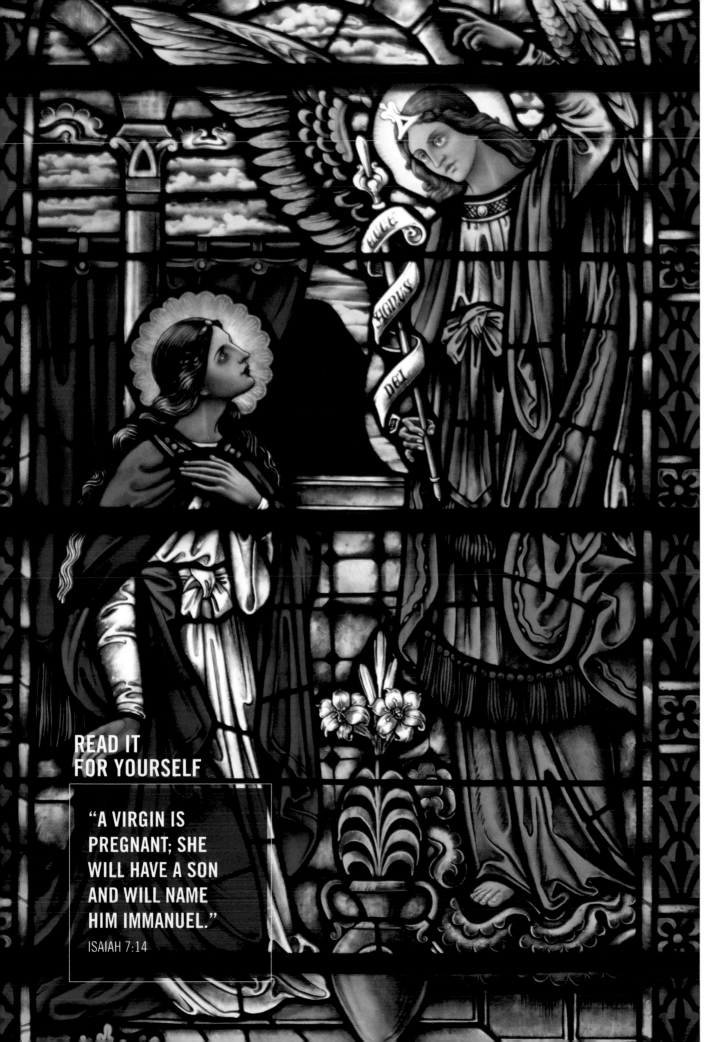

**READ IT
FOR YOURSELF**

"A VIRGIN IS
PREGNANT; SHE
WILL HAVE A SON
AND WILL NAME
HIM IMMANUEL."

ISAIAH 7:14

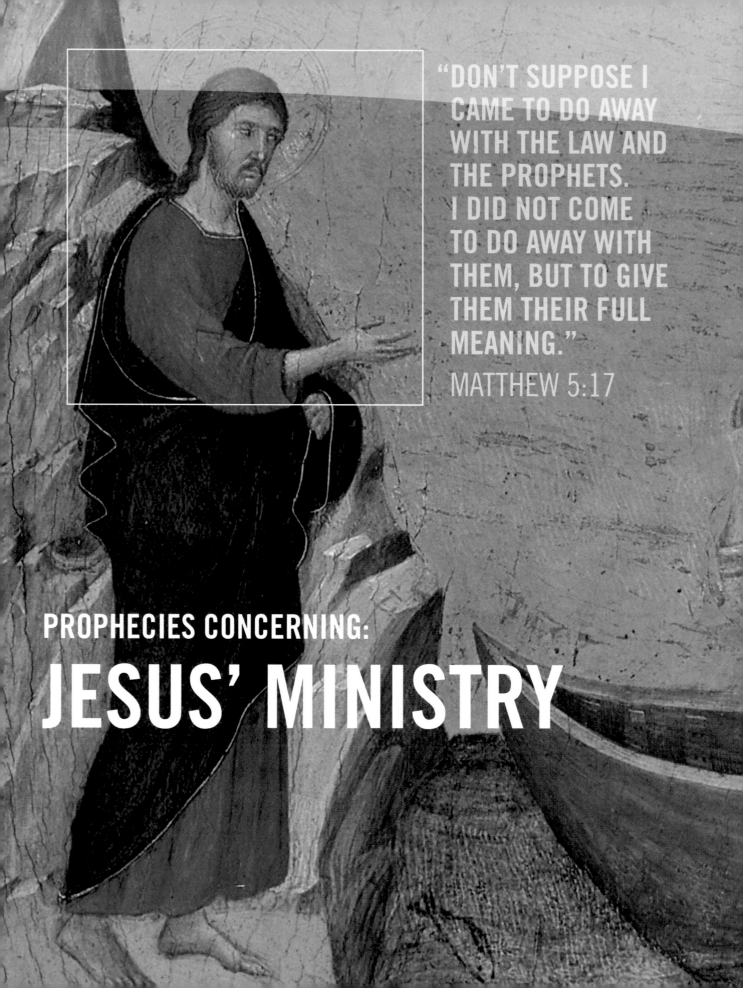

"DON'T SUPPOSE I CAME TO DO AWAY WITH THE LAW AND THE PROPHETS. I DID NOT COME TO DO AWAY WITH THEM, BUT TO GIVE THEM THEIR FULL MEANING."

MATTHEW 5:17

PROPHECIES CONCERNING:

JESUS' MINISTRY

5

JESUS' MINISTRY

REFERENCES TO JESUS' EARTHLY MINISTRY CALL TO MIND IMAGES OF ASTONISHING MIRACLES—TURNING WATER INTO WINE, HEALING THE SICK, RAISING THE DEAD. BUT MIRACLES ARE JUST ONE PART OF JESUS' STORY.

From the spectacular to the seemingly mundane, Jesus' actions were connected, at least in the minds of many of his followers, to the promises that God had made through ancient prophets about the one who would come in his name and champion his people. In the tradition of the prophet Jeremiah, who spoke of a new agreement God would make with his people (31:31-34), Jesus spoke of the new agreement that was forged by his shed blood and sacrificial death (Luke 22:20).

Everything about Jesus—his friends and colleagues, his teaching style, his attitude toward life and God—embodied the hopes of his ancestors and connected to prophetic tradition.

Not only was Jesus' life seen by many to fulfill prophecies, but Jesus was portrayed as a prophet by all four Gospels (Matthew 21:11, 46; Mark 6:15; Luke 7:16; 13:33; John 4:19; 6:14; 7:40; 9:17). The gospel writer Matthew, in particular, describes him as someone who spoke with the authority of a prophet (Matthew 7:29). Jesus himself even seems to confirm that portrayal by applying the proverb of a prophet being rejected in his hometown to himself (Matthew 13:57; Mark 6:4; Luke 4:24; John 4:44).

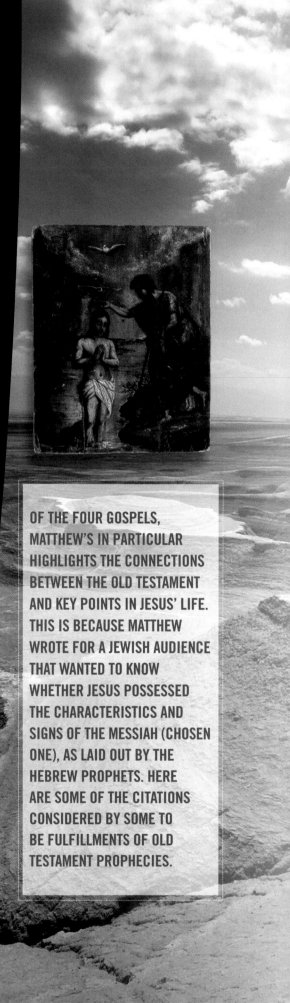

OF THE FOUR GOSPELS, MATTHEW'S IN PARTICULAR HIGHLIGHTS THE CONNECTIONS BETWEEN THE OLD TESTAMENT AND KEY POINTS IN JESUS' LIFE. THIS IS BECAUSE MATTHEW WROTE FOR A JEWISH AUDIENCE THAT WANTED TO KNOW WHETHER JESUS POSSESSED THE CHARACTERISTICS AND SIGNS OF THE MESSIAH (CHOSEN ONE), AS LAID OUT BY THE HEBREW PROPHETS. HERE ARE SOME OF THE CITATIONS CONSIDERED BY SOME TO BE FULFILLMENTS OF OLD TESTAMENT PROPHECIES.

VOICE IN THE WILDERNESS

Calling the World to Repentance

> **"I AM SENDING MY MESSENGER TO GET THE WAY READY FOR YOU. IN THE DESERT SOMEONE IS SHOUTING, 'GET THE ROAD READY FOR THE LORD! MAKE A STRAIGHT PATH FOR HIM.'"**
>
> MARK 1:2–3

Before Jesus went public—before he chose twelve disciples to travel with him and share his ministry—he had a kindred spirit in the man named John, who would become known as John the Baptist. Though he was a contemporary of Jesus, John is sometimes regarded as the last of the Old Testament-style prophets.

Jesus and John were part of an extended family. They may have known each other since childhood, if not from birth. When Mary learned she was pregnant, she immediately visited her relative Elizabeth, who was pregnant with John.

According to the account in Luke 1, when Mary and Elizabeth greeted each other, Elizabeth's unborn child moved inside her, prompting her to announce God's blessing on Mary's pregnancy. Elizabeth greeted Mary as "the mother of my Lord" (Luke 1:43).

The next time John appears in Luke's Gospel, we find him by the Jordan River, where John was preaching and baptizing. John's reputation as a fiery prophet was such that many wondered if he himself was the Messiah. But John seemed to have a singular purpose—to point the way to Jesus. He gladly drew attention away from himself and onto Jesus. He gave up his own disciples so they could follow Jesus. John saw himself as the fulfillment of Isaiah's prophecy; as someone whose sole purpose was to "get the road ready for the Lord."

OUR GOD HAS SAID: "ENCOURAGE MY PEOPLE! GIVE THEM COMFORT. SPEAK KINDLY TO JERUSALEM AND ANNOUNCE: YOUR SLAVERY IS PAST; YOUR PUNISHMENT IS OVER. I, THE LORD, MADE YOU PAY DOUBLE FOR YOUR SINS." SOMEONE IS SHOUTING: "CLEAR A PATH IN THE DESERT! MAKE A STRAIGHT ROAD FOR THE LORD OUR GOD. FILL IN THE VALLEYS; FLATTEN EVERY HILL AND MOUNTAIN. LEVEL THE ROUGH AND RUGGED GROUND. THEN THE GLORY OF THE LORD WILL APPEAR FOR ALL TO SEE. THE LORD HAS PROMISED THIS!" ISAIAH 40:1–5

ROOTS IN GALILEE

A Humble Beginning with a Great Promise

Galilee, a large region in northern Israel just west of Lake Galilee, takes center stage in much of Jesus' story. Many of the events described in the Gospels (particularly Matthew, Mark, and Luke) happened in or around Galilean towns such as Nazareth and Capernaum.

The prophets anticipated Galilee's role in the life of the Messiah. Centuries before Jesus, when the Israelites entered Canaan, they divided the land among the twelve tribal groups that comprised the nation. Two of those tribes were Zebulun and Naphtali, and their territory was the area later known as Galilee.

When the prophet Isaiah spoke of a bright light that would shine on people living in the darkest shadows, he alluded to the glory and honor destined for the territories of Zebulun and Naphtali. The Gospel writer Matthew referred back to Isaiah's prophecy (Matthew 4:13, 15-16), laying yet one more stone in the foundation of his contention that Jesus was indeed the Messiah spoken of by the prophets so many years before.

But Jesus was born in Bethlehem, many miles south of Galilee. Then his family fled to Egypt, escaping the wrath of Herod, Judea's paranoid king. After Herod died, however, Joseph acted on directions received in a dream and took Mary and Jesus to live in Nazareth, a small village in Galilee (see Matthew 2). Nazareth was the village where Joseph worked as a carpenter and where Mary and Joseph had lived before traveling to Bethlehem to participate in a Roman census (see Luke 1).

As an adult, Jesus maintained his "base of operations" in Galilee, but the nearby city of Capernaum, rather than Nazareth, became the hub of his mission. In fact, when Jesus made his well-known statement that prophets are not welcome in their own hometowns, he was speaking of Nazareth (Luke 4:24).

Synagogue ruins at Capernaum, Israel

■ *When Jesus heard that John had been put in prison, he went to Galilee. But instead of staying in Nazareth, Jesus moved to Capernaum. This town was beside Lake Galilee in the territory of Zebulun and Naphtali. So God's promise came true, just as the prophet Isaiah had said, "Listen, lands of Zebulun and Naphtali, lands along the road to the sea and across the Jordan. Listen Galilee, land of the Gentiles! Although your people live in darkness, they will see a bright light. Although they live in the shadow of death, a light will shine on them."*

Then Jesus started preaching, "Turn back to God! The kingdom of heaven will soon be here."

MATTHEW 4:12–17

"BUT THOSE WHO HAVE SUFFERED WILL NO LONGER BE IN PAIN. THE TERRITORIES OF ZEBULUN AND NAPHTALI IN GALILEE WERE ONCE HATED. BUT THIS LAND OF THE GENTILES ACROSS THE JORDAN RIVER AND ALONG THE MEDITERRANEAN SEA WILL BE GREATLY RESPECTED.

THOSE WHO WALKED IN THE DARK HAVE SEEN A BRIGHT LIGHT. AND IT SHINES UPON EVERYONE WHO LIVES IN THE LAND OF DARKEST SHADOWS." ISAIAH 9:1–2

A PASSIONATE DEFENDER OF GOD'S HOLY HOUSE

A Love for God That Burns Like a Fire

BIBLE PROPHECIES

The Gospels paint a remarkably human portrait of Jesus. He is a passionate figure, capable of expressing great love, amazement, and even anger.

One occasion when Jesus demonstrated real emotion was his clearing of the temple. What angered him was probably not the buying and selling that was taking place. After all, it was not unusual for animals to be sold at the temple. Often people traveled long distances and needed to buy animals for their sacrifices once they arrived in Jerusalem. But the moneychangers were turning a profit by converting people's coins into an "official" temple currency for their transactions. In doing so, they were most likely exploiting the poor and preventing non-Jewish worshipers from entering

the one space in the temple complex that had been reserved for them. This is what prompted Jesus' reaction.

As the disciples watched in surprise, an angry Jesus fashioned a homemade whip and drove the animals and the people out of the courtyard, overturning tables as he went. Then the disciples remembered something—a psalm that had come to be associated with the Messiah.

Psalm 69 is a prayer of David bemoaning those who hated him for no reason. In the midst of his prayer, David acknowledged his passion for God, a passion so great that when any insult was hurled at God, David took it as a personal affront (Psalm 69:8–9). David's words sprang to mind as Jesus took drastic measures to restore the

temple to its sacred purpose as a place of worship rather than profit. This association with King David, from whom the Messiah was to descend, shaped the disciples' understanding of Jesus' identity.

> **"I AM LIKE A STRANGER TO MY RELATIVES AND LIKE A FOREIGNER TO MY OWN FAMILY. MY LOVE FOR YOUR HOUSE BURNS IN ME LIKE A FIRE, AND WHEN OTHERS INSULT YOU, THEY INSULTED ME AS WELL."**
>
> PSALM 69:8–9

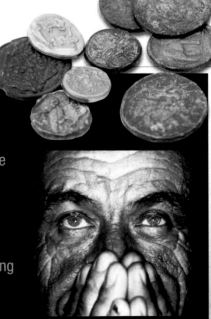

HAGGAI

Jesus' passion in clearing the temple reminded his followers of the words of Haggai, an Old Testament prophet who preached at the time after the Israelites had returned to Jerusalem after their long exile in Babylonia. At this low point of national and cultural pride, Haggai urged the Jews to rebuild Jerusalem's great temple, a symbol of unity and faith, as a sign that their nation was also finding the strength to rebuild itself.

"NOT LONG BEFORE THE JEWISH FESTIVAL OF PASSOVER, JESUS WENT TO JERUSALEM. THERE HE FOUND PEOPLE SELLING CATTLE, SHEEP, AND DOVES IN THE TEMPLE. HE ALSO SAW MONEYCHANGERS SITTING AT THEIR TABLES. SO HE TOOK SOME ROPE AND MADE A WHIP. THEN HE CHASED EVERYONE OUT OF THE TEMPLE, TOGETHER WITH THEIR SHEEP AND CATTLE. HE TURNED OVER THE TABLES OF THE MONEY-CHANGERS AND SCATTERED THEIR COINS.

JESUS SAID TO THE PEOPLE WHO HAD BEEN SELLING DOVES, 'GET THOSE DOVES OUT OF HERE! DON'T MAKE MY FATHER'S HOUSE A MARKETPLACE.'

THE DISCIPLES THEN REMEMBERED THAT THE SCRIPTURES SAY, 'MY LOVE FOR YOUR HOUSE BURNS IN ME LIKE A FIRE.'"

JOHN 2:13–17

LEADING BY SERVING

A Sacrifice that Defied Expectations

"THE SPIRIT OF THE LORD GOD HAS TAKEN CONTROL OF ME! THE LORD HAS CHOSEN AND SENT ME TO TELL THE OPPRESSED THE GOOD NEWS, TO HEAL THE BROKENHEARTED, AND TO ANNOUNCE FREEDOM FOR PRISONERS AND CAPTIVES. THIS IS THE YEAR WHEN THE LORD GOD WILL SHOW KINDNESS TO US AND PUNISH OUR ENEMIES. THE LORD HAS SENT ME TO COMFORT THOSE WHO MOURN."
ISAIAH 61:1–2

In the Gospels, Jesus demonstrated a revolutionary kind of leadership: *servant leadership*. Rather than present himself as a king and wait for people to serve him, Jesus came as a servant; one who cared for the needs of the sick, poor, and marginalized.

Perhaps the most poignant image of this divine humility is captured in the Gospel according to John. There Jesus literally put on the clothes and took the role of a servant just before his final Passover meal with his disciples.

Bending down, Jesus washed their feet—the lowest task that a household servant would have performed.

While Old Testament prophets like Isaiah anticipated the Messiah's humble form of leadership, it was far from what many of the people of Israel had in mind. They felt they needed a military champion, an aggressive warrior-king who could defeat the oppressive Roman Empire and end the military occupation in their land.

But Jesus had a different kind of strength. He was resolute in walking toward a sacrifice that would defy expectations and truly change the options available to those who shared his world. And so he did—quietly, humbly, and compassionately.

Jesus knew that he had come from God and would go back to God. He also knew that the Father had given him complete power. So during the meal Jesus got up, removed his outer garment, and wrapped a towel around his waist. He put some water into a large bowl. Then he began washing his disciples' feet and drying them with the towel he was wearing.

After Jesus had washed his disciples' feet and had put his outer garment back on, he sat down again. Then he said: Do you understand what I have done? You call me your teacher and Lord, and you should, because that is who I am. And if your Lord and teacher has washed your feet, you should do the same for each other. I have set the example, and you should do for each other exactly what I have done for you. I tell you for certain that servants are not greater than their master, and messengers are not greater than the one who sent them. You know these things, and God will bless you, if you do them.

JOHN 13:3–5, 12–17

ISAIAH

Isaiah was a well-educated prophet of the eighth century BC. His wife was also considered a prophetess, although she had no political or religious authority. While Isaiah walked the halls of power and served as an advisor to several Judean kings, he built his reputation as a social and political reformer.

In Christmas tradition, Isaiah also is famous for his poetic, majestic portrait of the long-awaited Messiah, whom he described in terms of suffering and obedience. It was from Isaiah's writings that now familiar expressions like "prince of peace" originated.

Some portions of Isaiah's prophecy are quite familiar because of their use in the lyrics of Handel's *Messiah*—for instance, Isaiah 53:4–6, which Handel quoted from the King James Version:

"Surely he hath borne our griefs, and carried our sorrows: yet we did esteem him stricken, smitten of God, and afflicted. But he was wounded for our transgressions, he was bruised for our iniquities: the chastisement of our peace was upon him; and with his stripes we are healed. All we like sheep have gone astray; we have turned every one to his own way; and the LORD hath laid on him the iniquity of us all."

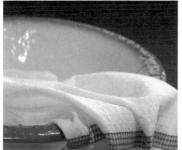

"HERE IS MY SERVANT! I HAVE MADE HIM STRONG. HE IS MY CHOSEN ONE; I AM PLEASED WITH HIM. I HAVE GIVEN HIM MY SPIRIT, AND HE WILL BRING JUSTICE TO THE NATIONS." ISAIAH 42:1

"THE LORD CARES FOR HIS NATION, JUST AS SHEPHERDS CARE FOR THEIR FLOCKS. HE CARRIES THE LAMBS IN HIS ARMS, WHILE GENTLY LEADING THE MOTHER SHEEP." ISAIAH 40:11

THE MIRACLES OF JESUS

WATER MADE WINE: JOHN 2:1–11

THE NOBLEMAN'S SON: JOHN 4:48–54

THE LACK OF FISH: LUKE 5:1–11

THE CURE OF THE DEMONIAC: MARK 1:23–28; LUKE 4:33–37

PETER'S MOTHER-IN-LAW: MATTHEW 8, 14–15; MARK 1, 29-31; LUKE 4:38–39

THE LEPER: MATTHEW 8:1–4; MARK 1:40–45; LUKE 5:12–19

THE PARALYTIC CURED: MATTHEW 9:1–8; MARK 2:1–12; LUKE 5:18–26

THE CURE AT BETHSAIDA: JOHN 5:1–15

THE WITHERED HAND: MATTHEW 12:9–13; MARK 3:1–6; LUKE 6:6–11

THE CENTURION'S SERVANT: MATTHEW 8:5–13; LUKE 7:2–10

THE WIDOW'S SON: LUKE 7:11–17

THE BLIND AND MUTE DEMONIAC: MATTHEW 12:22

THE STORM STILLED: MATTHEW 8:23–27; MARK 4:35–41; LUKE 8:22–25

EXPULSION OF DEVILS: MATTHEW 8:29–34; MARK 5:1–20; LUKE 8:26–39

JAIRUS'S DAUGHTER: MATTHEW 9:18–26; MARK 5:21–43; LUKE 8:40–56

THE WOMAN IN THE CROWD: MATTHEW 9:20–22; MARK 5:24–34; LUKE 8:43–48

TWO BLIND MEN: MATTHEW 9:27–31

THE MUTE SPIRIT: MATTHEW 9:32–34

FIVE THOUSAND FED: MATTHEW 14:13–21; MARK 6:34–44; LUKE 9:12–17; JOHN 6:1–15

JESUS WALKS ON THE WATER: MATTHEW 14:22–33; MARK 6:45–52; JOHN 6:16–21

THE CANAANITE WOMAN: MATTHEW 15:21–28; MARK 7:24–30

THE DEAF MUTE: MARK 7:31–37

FOUR THOUSAND FED: MATTHEW 15:32-38; MARK 8:1–9

THE BLIND MAN: MARK 8:22–25

THE POSSESSED BOY: MATTHEW 17:14–21; MARK 9:13–30; LUKE 9:37–43

TRIBUTE MONEY PROVIDED: MATTHEW 17:24–28

THE MAN BORN BLIND: JOHN 9:1–38

THE MUTE, LAME, AND BLIND: MATTHEW 15:29–31

 A WOMAN CURED: LUKE 13:10–17

THE MAN WITH THE DROPSY: LUKE 14:1–6

THE RAISING OF LAZARUS: JOHN 11:1–44

TEN LEPERS: LUKE 17:11–19

THE BLIND MEN AT JERICHO: MATTHEW 20:29–34; MARK 10:46–52; LUKE 18:35–43

THE FIG TREE BLASTED: MATTHEW 21:18–22; MARK 11:12–25

THE SERVANT'S EAR HEALED: LUKE 22:49–51

POOR FISHING: JOHN 21:1–14

THE MIRACULOUS

Healing the Blind, Deaf, Lame, Mute... and Other Divine Acts

The Old Testament prophet Isaiah promised a Messiah who would heal the blind, deaf, lame, and mute. The Gospels attribute many such miracles to Jesus. These were miracles of healing, divine acts of a Messiah who used his power for the benefit of others and to reveal God's glory. They reinforced the prophets' vision of a deliverer who would repair what was broken, heal the wounded, and restore the lost.

Yet, there were times when Jesus refused to do miracles. He pushed back against those who simply wanted a sign, a gimmick designed to impress them into believing. There were even some places where, according to the Gospels, Jesus could not perform many miracles because the inhabitants lacked faith.

Nevertheless, it was Jesus' miraculous activity—combined with the authority with which he spoke—that made people around him take notice and realize this was no ordinary man living among them, gathering followers, and offering hope.

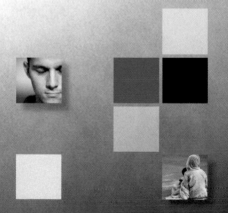

"DO YOU BELIEVE I CAN MAKE YOU WELL?"

AS JESUS WAS LEAVING THAT PLACE, TWO BLIND MEN BEGAN FOLLOWING HIM AND SHOUTING, "SON OF DAVID, HAVE PITY ON US!" AFTER JESUS HAD GONE INDOORS, THE TWO BLIND MEN CAME UP TO HIM. HE ASKED THEM, "DO YOU BELIEVE I CAN MAKE YOU WELL?"

"YES, LORD," THEY ANSWERED.

JESUS TOUCHED THEIR EYES AND SAID, "BECAUSE OF YOUR FAITH, YOU WILL BE HEALED." THEY WERE ABLE TO SEE, AND JESUS STRICTLY WARNED THEM NOT TO TELL ANYONE ABOUT HIM. BUT THEY LEFT AND TALKED ABOUT HIM TO EVERYONE IN THAT PART OF THE COUNTRY.

AS JESUS AND HIS DISCIPLES WERE ON THEIR WAY, SOME PEOPLE BROUGHT TO HIM A MAN WHO COULD NOT TALK BECAUSE A DEMON WAS IN HIM. AFTER JESUS HAD FORCED THE DEMON OUT, THE MAN STARTED TALKING. THE CROWDS WERE SO AMAZED THEY BEGAN SAYING, "NOTHING LIKE THIS HAS EVER HAPPENED IN ISRAEL!" MATTHEW 9:27–33

The deceased orant; healing of the man born blind; healing of the paralytic; healing of the bleeding woman. Detail of a frieze sarcophagus, marble high relief, Early Christian, ca. 300–325 CE. The last two scenes are an 18th-century integration by B. Cavaceppi.

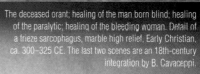

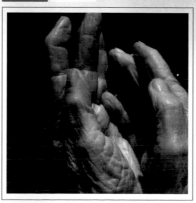

■ Here is a message for all who are weak, trembling, and worried: "Cheer up! Don't be afraid. Your God is coming to punish your enemies. God will take revenge on them and rescue you." The blind will see, and the ears of the deaf will be healed. Those who were lame will leap around like deer; tongues once silent will shout for joy. Water will rush through the desert. ISAIAH 35:3–6

"JESUS USED STORIES WHEN HE SPOKE TO THE PEOPLE. IN FACT, HE DID NOT TELL THEM ANYTHING WITHOUT USING STORIES. SO GOD'S PROMISE CAME TRUE, JUST AS THE PROPHET HAD SAID, 'I WILL USE STORIES TO SPEAK MY MESSAGE AND TO EXPLAIN THINGS HIDDEN SINCE THE CREATION OF THE WORLD.'" MATTHEW 13:34–35

STORIES THAT TEACH

Parables Revealing the Kingdom of God

Storytelling and riddles—also known as parables—were Jesus' favorite teaching device. Sometimes he explained the images and examples that he used; other times he did not. He didn't seem to mind simply telling stories that left his listeners pondering.

There may have been many reasons why Jesus used stories and examples from everyday life to illustrate his vision of the kingdom of God. The practice may have bought him time, masking the full implications of his teaching from angry religious leaders who wanted to undermine his ministry. Also, parables were effective in prompting his listeners to reflect more deeply on the core meaning of his teachings.

When asked by his own disciples why he taught with so many parables, Jesus cited Isaiah's description of those who could not see or understand the truth. Teaching in parables allowed Jesus to identify those who were discerning enough to "get" his message. He could reveal the secrets of God's kingdom in such a way that only those with the faith to embrace them would grasp their full meaning.

Jesus' disciples came to him and asked, "Why do you use stories to speak to the people?"

Jesus answered:
I have explained the secrets about the kingdom of heaven to you, but not to others. Everyone who has something will be given more. But people who don't have anything will lose even what little they have. I use stories when I speak to them because when they look, they cannot see, and when they listen, they cannot hear or understand. So God's promise came true, just as the prophet Isaiah had said,

"These people will listen and listen, but never understand. They will look and look, but never see. All of them have stubborn minds! They refuse to listen; they cover their eyes. They cannot see or hear or understand. If they could, they would turn to me, and I would heal them."

But God has blessed you, because your eyes can see and your ears can hear! Many prophets and good people were eager to see what you see and to hear what you hear. But I tell you they did not see or hear.

MATTHEW 13:10–17

SELECTED PROPHECIES CONCERNING THE MESSIAH AND THEIR FULFILLMENT

Listed below are selected Bible prophecies that Christians have interpreted as referring to the Messiah. In the left-hand column, you'll find the reference to the prophecy. In the right-hand column, you'll find a reference to its fulfillment. This list maintains the order in which the prophecies appear in the Bible.

OLD TESTAMENT PROHECY	WHAT THE PROPHECY REVEALS ABOUT THE MESSIAH	NEW TESTAMENT FULFILLMENT
Genesis 3:15	He will be the offspring of a woman and defeat Satan.	Galatians 4:4–5; Revelation 12:11
Genesis 12:1–3 (see also Genesis 21:12; 22:18)	He will be a descendant of Abraham and Isaac.	Galatians 3:16; Hebrews 11:17–19; Matthew 1:1, 17
Exodus 12:46 (see also Psalm 34:20)	He will not have any of his bones broken.	John 19:33,36
Deuteronomy 18:15–18	He will be a prophet like Moses.	Acts 3:20–22
Psalm 2:1–2,6–7	He will be opposed by both Jews and Gentiles. He will be King of Zion and the Son of God.	Luke 1:32,35; 23:10–12; John 18:33–37; Acts 4:27
Psalm 16:10 (see also Psalm 30:3)	His body will not decay in the grave.	Luke 24:6,31,34; Acts 2:31
Psalm 22:1–18	He will be forsaken by God, mocked by people, and have his clothing divided by the casting of dice.	Matthew 27:39–44,46; Luke 22:63–65; John 19:18–20,23–24; Romans 15:3
Psalm 41:9 (see also Psalm 55:12–14)	He will be betrayed by a friend.	Matthew 26:14–16; Mark 14:10–11; Luke 22:1–6; John 13:18,21–30
Psalm 47:5	He will ascend into heaven.	Luke 24:51; Acts 1:9
Psalm 69:21	He will be offered gall and vinegar to drink.	Matthew 27:34; Mark 15:36; Luke 23:36; John 19:29–30
Psalm 69:4	He will be rejected and hated for his works.	Matthew 13:57; Mark 6:4; Luke 4:24; John 1:11; 7:3–5; 15:24–25
Psalm 69:9	He will have great love for the Lord's house.	John 2:17
Psalm 72:10–11 (see also Psalm 72:8; Daniel 7:14)	He will be adored by great people. He will have universal dominion.	Matthew 2:1–11; Philippians 2:9,11
Psalm 78:2	He will preach in parables.	Matthew 13:34–35; Mark 4:33–34
Psalm 110:1 (see also Psalm 2:7; 110:4)	He will sit at the right hand of God. He will serve in Melchizedek's order of priests.	Hebrews 1:3; 5:5–6; Colossians 3:1
Psalm 118:22	He will be rejected by Jewish rulers.	Matthew 21:42; Mark 12:10; Luke 20:17; 1 Peter 2:4–7
Isaiah 7:14	He will be born of a virgin.	Matthew 1:21–23; Luke 2:7
Isaiah 8:14	He will be a stumbling block to those who refuse to believe in him.	Luke 2:34; Romans 9:32–33; 1 Peter 2:8
Isaiah 9:1–2,7 (see also Daniel 7:14)	He will have a ministry that begins in Galilee. He will have an everlasting kingdom.	Matthew 4:12–16,23; Luke 1:32–33
Isaiah 11:10; 42:1 (see also Isaiah 56:6–8)	He will have Gentile followers.	John 10:16; Acts 10:34–35, 45, 47
Isaiah 28:16	He will be the chief cornerstone of God's people.	1 Peter 2:6–7

Concerning the Messiah

OLD TESTAMENT PROHECY	WHAT THE PROPHECY REVEALS ABOUT THE MESSIAH	NEW TESTAMENT FULFILLMENT
Isaiah 35:5–6	He will perform miracles.	Matthew 11:4–6; John 9:6, 7
Isaiah 40:3 (see also Malachi 3:1)	He will be preceded by an anointed messenger.	Matthew 3:13; Mark 1:2–3; Luke 1:17,76–77; 3:3-6; John 1:23
Isaiah 42:1–6	He will be meek and speak out for justice.	Matthew 12:15–21
Isaiah 50:6 (see also Isaiah 52:14)	He will be spat on and beaten.	Matthew 26:67; Mark 14:65; 15:19; John 19:1–5
Isaiah 53:1–12	He will be condemned as a sinner and will suffer. He will be silent before his accusers (and later intercede for them), and be buried with the rich.	Matthew 26:62–63; 27:11–14, 27–50, 57–60; Mark 15:4–5, 21–37, 42-46; Luke 23:6–9, 32-46, 50–54; John 19:16–30, 38–42; 1 Peter 2:22
Isaiah 61:1 (see also Isaiah 11:2)	He will be anointed by the Spirit of God.	Matthew 3:16; Mark 1:10; Luke 3:22; Luke 4:16-19; John 3:34; 5:30; Acts 10:38; Revelation 19:11
Isaiah 61:1–2	He will enter public ministry.	Luke 4:16–21,43
Jeremiah 23:5–6 (see also Jeremiah 33:14–16)	He will be a descendant of David.	Matthew 1:1, 17; Acts 13:22–23; Romans 1:3
Jeremiah 31:15	He will be alive during the slaughter of Bethlehem's children.	Matthew 2:16–18
Hosea 11:1	He will be called out of Egypt.	Matthew 2:15
Micah 5:2–5	He will be born in Bethlehem.	Matthew 2:1–6; Luke 2:4–7
Malachi 3:1	He will arrive at Jerusalem's temple.	Matthew 21:12; Mark 11:11; Luke 19:45–48; John 2:13–16
Zechariah 9:9	He will enter Jerusalem by riding a donkey.	Matthew 21:1–5
Zechariah 11:12–13	He will be betrayed for thirty pieces of silver, which will later buy a potter's field.	Matthew 26:15; 27:7
Zechariah 12:10	He will be pierced.	John 19:34,37
Zechariah 13:7	He will be forsaken by his disciples.	Matthew 26:31,56

"IF JOSHUA HAD REALLY GIVEN PEOPLE REST, THERE WOULD NOT BE ANY NEED FOR GOD TO TALK ABOUT ANOTHER DAY OF REST. BUT GOD HAS PROMISED US A SABBATH WHEN WE WILL REST, EVEN THOUGH IT HAS NOT YET COME. ON THAT DAY GOD'S PEOPLE WILL REST FROM THEIR WORK, JUST AS GOD RESTED FROM HIS WORK." HEBREWS 4:8–10

IN GOOD COMPANY

The Ultimate Prophet, Priest, and King

The Gospel writers believed that Jesus had come to fulfill all the key roles that were sacred to ancient Israel. He was, in effect, the ultimate prophet, priest, and king.

As prophet, Jesus was God's messenger, bringing divine truth to people. As priest, Jesus interceded on their behalf, connecting them to God. And as king, he would lead them into the glory God had promised them and be their protector.

The Old Testament points to the Messiah as the fulfillment of these roles—comparing him to significant forebears in faith like Moses, Melchizedek, and Joshua.

The prophets said that the Messiah would be a prophet like Moses, the one who received the Ten Commandments and communicated God's Law to the people. Jesus repeatedly highlighted his relationship to the Law and the Prophets, saying that he came to fulfill rather than do away with them (Matthew 5:17).

The New Testament book of Hebrews describes Jesus as a high priest, comparing him to a little-known, yet important, man named Melchizedek, an Old Testament priest from the time of Abraham (Hebrews 7; cf. Genesis 14:18–20). Just as God declared Melchizedek a high priest and permanent son within God's family, so, too, Jesus would take the role of high priest—forever.

Though not a king in the formal sense, Joshua led the Israelites during one of the most critical periods in their history: the conquest of Canaan. After the Israelites settled in the land of Canaan, Joshua spoke words of peace to the people. Yet, because enemies of Israel still surrounded them, peace would not continue indefinitely. In the letter to the Hebrews, the writer speaks of God's promised eternal rest for those who put their faith in Jesus.

A PRIEST FOREVER

"THIS IS HOW IT WAS WITH CHRIST. HE BECAME A HIGH PRIEST, BUT NOT JUST BECAUSE HE WANTED THE HONOR OF BEING ONE. IT WAS GOD WHO TOLD HIM, 'YOU ARE MY SON, BECAUSE TODAY I HAVE BECOME YOUR FATHER!' IN ANOTHER PLACE, GOD SAYS, 'YOU ARE A PRIEST FOREVER JUST LIKE MELCHIZEDEK.'

SUFFERING MADE JESUS PERFECT, AND NOW HE CAN SAVE FOREVER ALL WHO OBEY HIM. THIS IS BECAUSE GOD CHOSE HIM TO BE A HIGH PRIEST LIKE MELCHIZEDEK."

HEBREWS 5:5–6, 9–10

Moses said to Israel:

■ *Instead, he will choose one of your own people to be a prophet just like me, and you must do what that prophet says. You were asking for a prophet the day you were gathered at Mount Sinai and said to the LORD, "Please don't let us hear your voice or see this terrible fire again—if we do, we will die!" Then the LORD told me:*

Moses, they have said the right thing. So when I want to speak to them, I will choose one of them to be a prophet like you. I will give my message to that prophet, who will tell the people exactly what I have said. DEUTERONOMY 18:15–18

■ *Joshua held a meeting with the men of the tribes of Reuben, Gad, and East Manasseh, and he told them:*

You have obeyed every command of the LORD your God and of his servant Moses. And you have done everything I've told you to do. It's taken a long time, but you have stayed and helped your relatives.

The LORD promised to give peace to your relatives, and that's what he has done. Now it's time for you to go back to your own homes in the land that Moses gave you east of the Jordan River. JOSHUA 22:1–4

MELCHISEDEC

THE TRIUMPHAL ENTRY

Blessed Is He Who Comes in the Name of the Lord!

> "EVERYONE IN JERUSALEM, CELEBRATE AND SHOUT! YOUR KING HAS WON A VICTORY, AND HE IS COMING TO YOU. HE IS HUMBLE AND RIDES ON A DONKEY; HE COMES ON THE COLT OF A DONKEY."
>
> ZECHARIAH 9:9

For many of us, the story of Easter begins with Jesus' "triumphal entry" into Jerusalem one week before his execution on a cross. He was traveling with his disciples to celebrate the Passover feast, and as they approached the holy city, he told them to go to a nearby village and borrow a donkey for him to ride. It may seem a bizarre turn of events—but it was orchestrated to fulfill yet another prophecy about the Messiah.

Zechariah told everyone to "celebrate and shout" because their savior would come to Jerusalem, humble and riding on a donkey (Zechariah 9:9). Much fanfare greeted Jesus upon his arrival in Jerusalem. The waving of palm branches and the shouts of "Blessed is the king who comes in the name of the Lord," echoed the words of Psalm 118:26–27.

The Gospel accounts of the triumphal entry take on a deeper meaning when we understand the significance that the donkey, the celebration, and the setting would have held for those watching. They were signs that the one riding on the donkey was indeed their Messiah. Jesus acknowledged the importance of this moment when he confidently rebuked the Pharisees who found the whole scene rather blasphemous. Jesus told them that the very rocks would cry out if the people were silenced.

> "GOD BLESS THE ONE WHO COMES IN THE NAME OF THE LORD! WE PRAISE YOU HERE IN THE HOUSE OF THE LORD. THE LORD IS OUR GOD, AND HE HAS GIVEN US LIGHT! START THE CELEBRATION! MARCH WITH PALM BRANCHES ALL THE WAY TO THE ALTAR." PSALM 118:26–27

■ As [Jesus] was getting near Bethphage and Bethany on the Mount of Olives, he sent two of his disciples on ahead. He told them, "Go into the next village, where you will find a young donkey that has never been ridden. Untie the donkey and bring it here. If anyone asks why you are doing this, just say, 'The Lord needs it.' " They went off and found everything just as Jesus had said. While they were untying the donkey, its owners asked, "Why are you doing that?"

They answered, "The Lord needs it."

Then they led the donkey to Jesus. They put some of their clothes on its back and helped Jesus get on. And as he rode along, the people spread clothes on the road in front of him. When Jesus started down the Mount of Olives, his large crowd of disciples were happy and praised God because of all the miracles they had seen.
They shouted,
"Blessed is the king who comes
in the name of the Lord!
Peace in heaven
and glory to God."

Some Pharisees in the crowd said to Jesus, "Teacher, make your disciples stop shouting!"

But Jesus answered, "If they keep quiet, these stones will start shouting."

When Jesus came closer and could see Jerusalem, he cried and said:
"It is too bad that today your people don't know what will bring them peace! Now it is hidden from them. Jerusalem, the time will come when your enemies will build walls around you to attack you. Armies will surround you and close in on you from every side. They will level you to the ground and kill your people. Not one stone in your buildings will be left on top of another. This will happen because you did not see that God had come to save you."

LUKE 19:29–44

JESUS REVEALS HIS IDENTITY

The Fulfillment of the Old Testament Messiah

Throughout his ministry, Jesus turned to the prophets to reveal to others who he understood himself to be. These statements of self-authentication were his way of assuring his listeners that he had come to fulfill the law of the Old Testament.

One of the most striking examples was his reading of scripture in the synagogue at Nazareth, his home-town. The scripture was from Isaiah, a passage closely associated by many with the promised Messiah. Upon reading the powerful words—that he had come to announce freedom and bring sight to the blind—Jesus made an even more pointed statement. As the crowd fixed their eyes on him, he announced that Isaiah's prophecy had come true then and there (Luke 4:16–21). This was a bold move.

There were other occasions when Jesus appeared to confirm his identity as the Messiah. In his well-known conversation with a Samaritan woman, he spoke candidly about being the Messiah that she was looking for (John 4:19–26). In conversations with his disciples, Jesus explained events like Judas's betrayal by saying it was necessary to fulfill Old Testament prophecies.

In retrospect—and with the advantage of a historical perspective—Jesus seemed rather straightforward about his identity and his connection with the hope of the ancients.

JESUS WENT BACK TO NAZARETH, WHERE HE HAD BEEN BROUGHT UP, AND AS USUAL HE WENT TO THE SYNAGOGUE ON THE SABBATH. WHEN HE STOOD UP TO READ FROM THE SCRIPTURES, HE WAS GIVEN THE BOOK OF ISAIAH THE PROPHET. HE OPENED IT AND READ,

"THE LORD'S SPIRIT HAS COME TO ME, BECAUSE HE HAS CHOSEN ME TO TELL THE GOOD NEWS TO THE POOR. THE LORD HAS SENT ME TO ANNOUNCE FREEDOM FOR PRISONERS, TO GIVE SIGHT TO THE BLIND, TO FREE EVERYONE WHO SUFFERS, AND TO SAY, 'THIS IS THE YEAR THE LORD HAS CHOSEN....'"

THEN JESUS SAID TO THEM, "WHAT YOU HAVE JUST HEARD ME READ HAS COME TRUE TODAY." LUKE 4:16–21

When Jesus and his disciples were near the town of Caesarea Philippi, he asked them, "What do people say about the Son of Man?"

The disciples answered, "Some people say you are John the Baptist or maybe Elijah or Jeremiah or some other prophet." Then Jesus asked, "But who do you say I am?"

Simon Peter spoke up, "You are the Messiah, the Son of the living God."

Jesus told him: Simon, son of Jonah, you are blessed! You didn't discover this on your own. It was shown to you by my Father in heaven. So I will call you Peter, which means "a rock." On this rock I will build my church, and death itself will not have any power over it. I will give you the keys to the kingdom of heaven, and God in heaven will allow whatever you allow on earth. But he will not allow anything that you don't allow.

MATTHEW 16:13–19

The woman said, "Sir, I can see that you are a prophet. My ancestors worshiped on this mountain, but you Jews say Jerusalem is the only place to worship." Jesus said to her:

Believe me, the time is coming when you won't worship the Father either on this mountain or in Jerusalem. You Samaritans don't really know the one you worship. But we Jews do know the God we worship, and by using us, God will save the world. But a time is coming, and it is already here! Even now the true worshipers are being led by the Spirit to worship the Father according to the truth. These are the ones the Father is seeking to worship him. God is Spirit, and those who worship God must be led by the Spirit to worship him according to the truth.

The woman said, "I know that the Messiah will come. He is the one we call Christ. When he comes, he will explain everything to us."

"I am that one," Jesus told her, "and I am speaking to you now."

JOHN 4:19–26

BUT WHO DO YOU SAY I AM?

PROPHETIC COUNTDOWN

Questioning the End of Human History

[JESUS SAID,] "WE ARE NOW ON OUR WAY TO JERUSALEM, WHERE THE SON OF MAN WILL BE HANDED OVER TO THE CHIEF PRIESTS AND THE TEACHERS OF THE LAW OF MOSES. THEY WILL SENTENCE HIM TO DEATH, AND THEN THEY WILL HAND HIM OVER TO FOREIGNERS WHO WILL MAKE FUN OF HIM. THEY WILL BEAT HIM AND NAIL HIM TO A CROSS. BUT ON THE THIRD DAY HE WILL RISE FROM DEATH." MATTHEW 20:18–19

In addition to quoting Old Testament prophets, Jesus spoke a few prophecies of his own. On more than one occasion he predicted his own death. He also spoke of a time when he would return to earth to inaugurate events associated with the final judgment and the coming of a new heaven and earth.

When pressed by his disciples, Jesus explained at length the unpredictable nature of these "end times" events. He claimed no one knew but God himself when they would take place (Matthew 24). While the book of Revelation, with its symbols and visions, is an apocalyptic book of the New Testament with close ties to the prophetic books in the Old Testament, Jesus' teachings included their own description of the mysterious events surrounding the end of history as we know it.

WHAT'S THE SIGN OF YOUR COMING?

■ Later, as Jesus was sitting on the Mount of Olives, his disciples came to him in private and asked, "When will this happen? What will be the sign of your coming and of the end of the world?"

Jesus answered:

Don't let anyone fool you. Many will

You will soon hear about wars and threats of wars, but don't be afraid. These things will have to happen first, but that isn't the end. Nations and kingdoms will go to war against each other. People will starve to death, and in some places there will be earthquakes. But this is just the beginning of troubles.

You will be arrested, punished, and even killed. Because of me, you will be hated by people of all nations. Many will give up and will betray and hate each other. Many false prophets will come and fool a lot of people. Evil will spread and cause many people to stop loving others. But if you keep on being faithful right to the end, you will be saved. When the good news about the kingdom has been preached all over the world and told to all nations,

Someday you will see that "Horrible Thing" in the holy place, just as the prophet Daniel said. Everyone who reads this must try to understand! If you are living in Judea at that time, run to the mountains. If you are on the roof of your house, don't go inside to get anything. If you are out in the field, don't go back for your coat. It will be a terrible time for women who are expecting babies or nursing young children. And pray that you won't have to escape in winter or on a Sabbath. This will be the worst time of suffering since the beginning of the world, and nothing this terrible will ever happen again. If God doesn't make the time shorter, no one will be left alive. But because of God's chosen ones, he will make the time shorter. Someone may say, "Here is the Messiah!" or "There he is!" But

even try to fool God's chosen ones. But I have warned you ahead of time. If you are told that the Messiah is out in the desert, don't go there! And if you are told that he is in some secret place, don't believe it! The coming of the Son of Man will be like lightning that can be seen from east to west. Where there is a corpse, there will always be vultures.

*Right after those days of suffering,
"The sun will become dark,
and the moon
will no longer shine.
The stars will fall,
and the powers in the sky will be shaken."*

Then a sign will appear in the sky. And there will be the Son of Man. All nations on earth will weep when

trumpet, he will send his angels to bring his chosen ones together from all over the earth.

Learn a lesson from a fig tree. When its branches sprout and start putting out leaves, you know that summer is near. So when you see all these things happening, you will know that the time has almost come. I can promise you that some of the people of this generation will still be alive when all this happens. The sky and the earth won't last forever, but my words will.

No one knows the day or hour. The angels in heaven don't know, and the Son himself doesn't know. Only the Father knows. When the Son of Man appears, things will be just as they were when Noah lived. People were

boat. They didn't know anything was happening until the flood came and swept them all away. That is how it will be when the Son of Man appears. Two men will be in the same field, but only one will be taken. The other will be left. Two women will be together grinding grain, but only one will be taken. The other will be left. So be on your guard! You don't know when your Lord will come. Homeowners never know when a thief is coming, and they are always on guard to keep one from breaking in. Always be ready! You don't know when the Son of Man will come.

MATTHEW 24:3–44

PROPHECIES CONCERNING:

JESUS' DEATH AND RESURRECTION

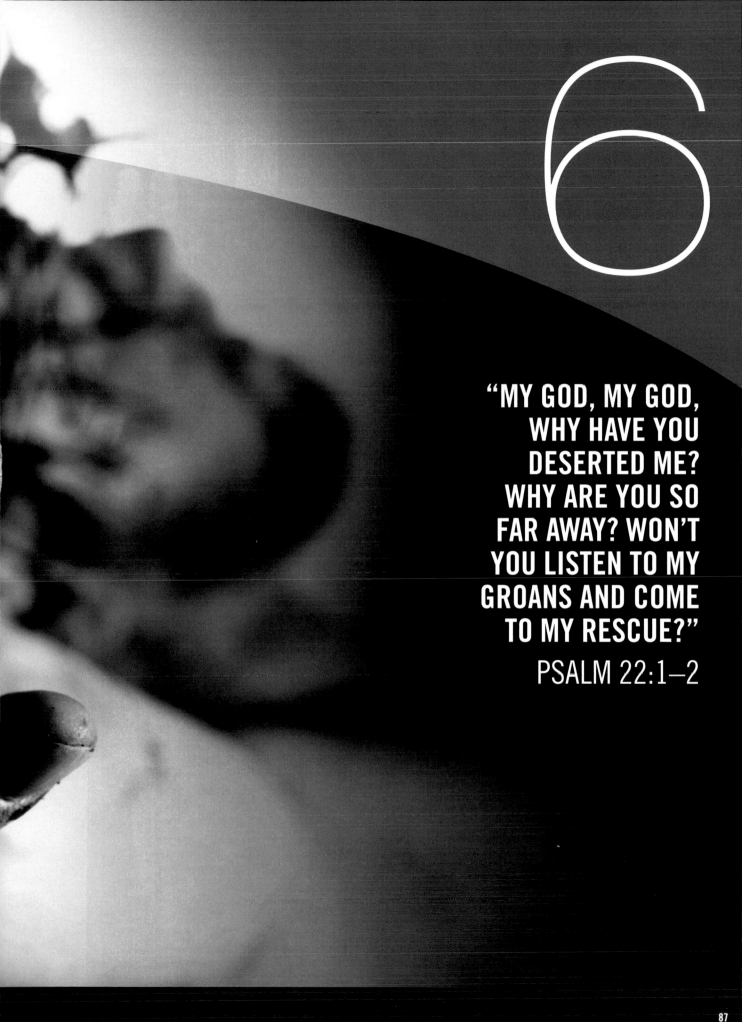

6

"MY GOD, MY GOD, WHY HAVE YOU DESERTED ME? WHY ARE YOU SO FAR AWAY? WON'T YOU LISTEN TO MY GROANS AND COME TO MY RESCUE?"

PSALM 22:1–2

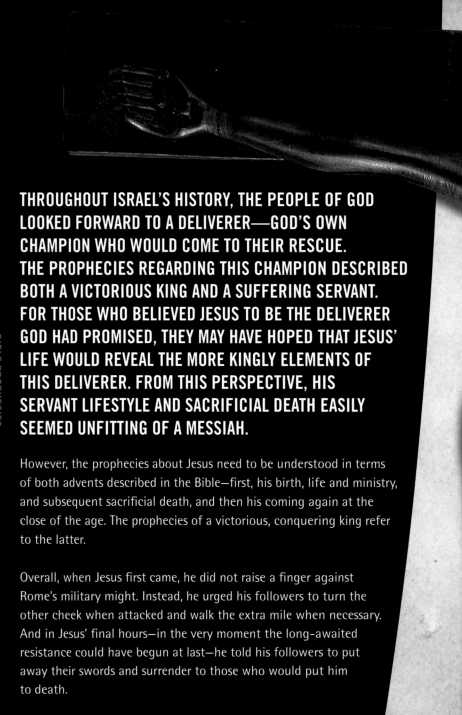

THROUGHOUT ISRAEL'S HISTORY, THE PEOPLE OF GOD LOOKED FORWARD TO A DELIVERER—GOD'S OWN CHAMPION WHO WOULD COME TO THEIR RESCUE. THE PROPHECIES REGARDING THIS CHAMPION DESCRIBED BOTH A VICTORIOUS KING AND A SUFFERING SERVANT. FOR THOSE WHO BELIEVED JESUS TO BE THE DELIVERER GOD HAD PROMISED, THEY MAY HAVE HOPED THAT JESUS' LIFE WOULD REVEAL THE MORE KINGLY ELEMENTS OF THIS DELIVERER. FROM THIS PERSPECTIVE, HIS SERVANT LIFESTYLE AND SACRIFICIAL DEATH EASILY SEEMED UNFITTING OF A MESSIAH.

However, the prophecies about Jesus need to be understood in terms of both advents described in the Bible—first, his birth, life and ministry, and subsequent sacrificial death, and then his coming again at the close of the age. The prophecies of a victorious, conquering king refer to the latter.

Overall, when Jesus first came, he did not raise a finger against Rome's military might. Instead, he urged his followers to turn the other cheek when attacked and walk the extra mile when necessary. And in Jesus' final hours—in the very moment the long-awaited resistance could have begun at last—he told his followers to put away their swords and surrender to those who would put him to death.

A FRIEND'S BETRAYAL

When Judas, one of Jesus' disciples, betrayed Jesus for thirty pieces of silver, his deception carried not just the sting of abandonment, but the echo of several Old Testament prophecies pointing toward just such an unthinkable turn of events. In anticipation of his disciple's treachery, Jesus quoted his ancestor King David lamenting the betrayal of a friend who once ate from the same table (see Psalm 41:9). Psalm 55:12–23 expressed similar heartbreak in response to a friend-turned-enemy—precisely what happened when Judas betrayed Jesus.

In the Jewish culture, sharing a meal carried special significance—and expectations—in terms of hospitality, loyalty, and even protection. According to the Gospel accounts, Judas shared the most important meal of Jesus' life—what is often referred to as the Last Supper—shortly before revealing Jesus' identity to his enemies. Thus, in betraying Jesus, he violated both his friend's trust and the customs of hospitality. And he did so for a pittance.

One of Zechariah's prophecies foreshadowed the sum Judas was paid for his betrayal—thirty pieces of silver (Zechariah 11:12–13). Even in ancient times, this was not considered a significant amount. Zechariah underscores this fact, calling the payment "measly" and suggesting that it be thrown into the temple's treasury. According to Matthew, once Judas realized that Jesus was going to be put to death, he regretted what he had done and tried to return the money, throwing it into the treasury. But realizing it was too late to undo what he had done, Judas went out and hanged himself (Matthew 27:3–5). The book of Acts (1:18) reports that Judas died by throwing himself over a cliff.

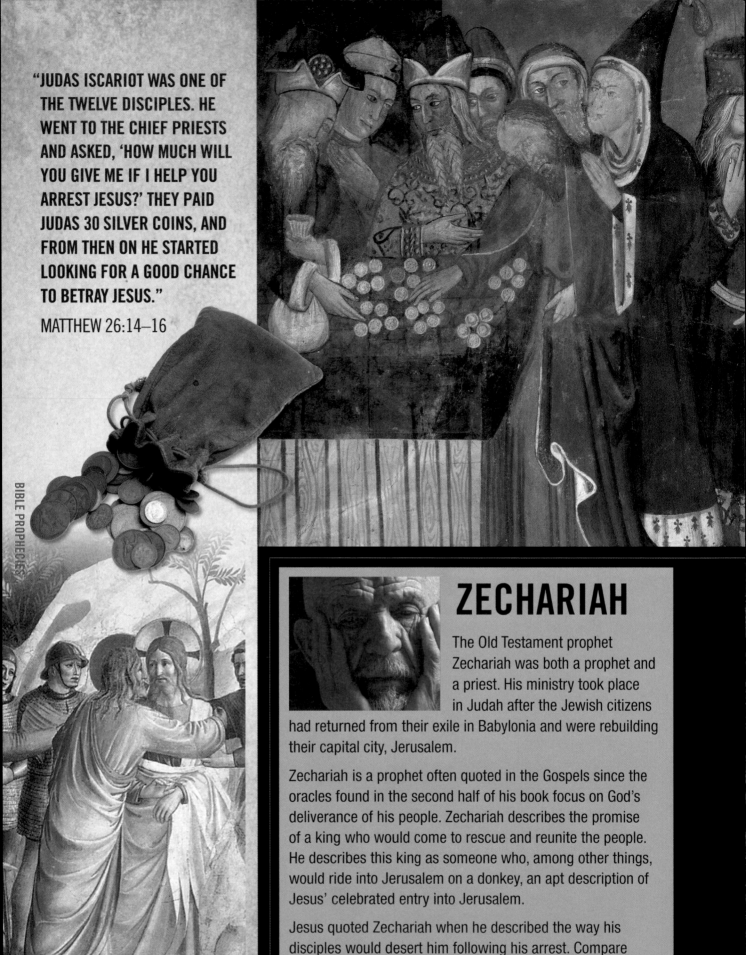

"JUDAS ISCARIOT WAS ONE OF THE TWELVE DISCIPLES. HE WENT TO THE CHIEF PRIESTS AND ASKED, 'HOW MUCH WILL YOU GIVE ME IF I HELP YOU ARREST JESUS?' THEY PAID JUDAS 30 SILVER COINS, AND FROM THEN ON HE STARTED LOOKING FOR A GOOD CHANCE TO BETRAY JESUS."

MATTHEW 26:14–16

ZECHARIAH

The Old Testament prophet Zechariah was both a prophet and a priest. His ministry took place in Judah after the Jewish citizens had returned from their exile in Babylonia and were rebuilding their capital city, Jerusalem.

Zechariah is a prophet often quoted in the Gospels since the oracles found in the second half of his book focus on God's deliverance of his people. Zechariah describes the promise of a king who would come to rescue and reunite the people. He describes this king as someone who, among other things, would ride into Jerusalem on a donkey, an apt description of Jesus' celebrated entry into Jerusalem.

Jesus quoted Zechariah when he described the way his disciples would desert him following his arrest. Compare Zechariah 13:7–9 with Mark 14:27.

DESERTED AND ALONE

The writings of Zechariah hinted not only at the payment of thirty silver pieces; they also anticipated other details about a Shepherd of Israel who was to come.

This reference to a shepherd was a familiar one in this culture and thus effective. In the Old Testament, kings and other leaders were sometimes described as shepherds (see Jeremiah 23:1-4; Ezekiel 34). Numbers 27:16–17 describes a people that need a leader so that they do not wander around like sheep without a shepherd.

In Zechariah's case, he spoke of a shepherd that would be struck down (Zechariah 13:7). His words were not understood as a prophetic description of the coming Messiah until Jesus himself quoted them during his final meal with his followers (Mark 14:27).

The prophecy describes quite simply what happens to sheep when their shepherd is struck—they scatter. Jesus' disciples fared no better following his arrest. During his time of greatest trial and suffering, his followers abandoned him and scattered like sheep.

The fulfillment of this prophecy was recorded in all four Gospels. Peter's promise not to betray Jesus (Matthew 26:31–35; Mark 14:27–31; Luke 22:31–34; John 13:36–38), and the rooster's crowing that served as a painful reminder of his failure to keep that pledge, is perhaps the most

vivid and tragic example of how the disciples scattered during this crucial moment in Jesus' life. Elsewhere, John described how only Jesus' favorite disciple, Jesus' mother, Mary, and several other women remained at Jesus' side through the ordeal of the crucifixion (John 19:25–27).

Yet even in the midst of abandonment, Jesus offered his disciples peace and promised that the Father would be with him even after each of them had deserted him (John 16:31–33).

■ Matthew 27:3–5

Judas had betrayed Jesus, but when he learned that Jesus had been sentenced to death, he was sorry for what he had done. He returned the 30 silver coins to the chief priests and leaders and said, "I have sinned by betraying a man who has never done anything wrong."

"So what? That's your problem," they replied. Judas threw the money into the temple and then went out and hanged himself.

> "THE LORD ALL-POWERFUL SAID: 'MY SWORD, WAKE UP! ATTACK MY SHEPHERD AND FRIEND. STRIKE DOWN THE SHEPHERD! SCATTER THE LITTLE SHEEP, AND I WILL DESTROY THEM.'"
> ZECHARIAH 13:7

above: *Scenes from the life of Jesus Christ: Payment of Judas*
15th century, Chapelle St. Antoine, Bessans, France

left: *The Kiss of Judas*
1442, Fra Angelico

THE SILENCE OF THE LAMB

Ecce Homo, 1871
Antonio Ciseri (1821–91)

Acts 8:31–35

The official answered, "How can I understand unless someone helps me?" He then invited Philip to come up and sit beside him. The man was reading the passage that said, "He was led like a sheep on its way to be killed. He was silent as a lamb whose wool is being cut off, and he did not say a word. He was treated like a nobody and did not receive a fair trial. How can he have children, if his life is snatched away?" The official said to Philip, "Tell me, was the prophet talking about himself or about someone else?" So Philip began at this place in the Scriptures and explained the good news about Jesus.

While Isaiah 52:13–53:12 and the other Servant Songs of Isaiah (42:1–4; 49:1–6; 50:4–9) are often seen as pointing to God's people, the Israelites, Christian tradition has interpreted them as a description of the coming Messiah—the one who will save God's people. So why did Isaiah picture a lamb being led to slaughter? It just doesn't seem to fit the image of a mighty savior or king. Yet when Jesus was put on trial by Pontius Pilate before an angry crowd, the picture painted by Isaiah became all too real.

Christ before Pilate
Mihály Munkácsy, 1881

"PILATE ASKED HIM, 'DON'T YOU HEAR WHAT CRIMES THEY SAY YOU HAVE DONE?' BUT JESUS DID NOT SAY ANYTHING, AND THE GOVERNOR WAS GREATLY AMAZED."
MATTHEW 27:13–14

The Gospels recount the fulfillment of Isaiah's words, describing in detail how Jesus suffered abuse while neither protesting the accusations hurled his way nor even bothering to answer the charges against him (Matthew 27:11–14; Mark 15:2–5; Luke 23:3–5; John 18:33–38). When Pilate, the Roman governor, demanded that Jesus address the charges, Jesus responded by silently fulfilling Isaiah's prophecy.

Some time after Jesus' death and resurrection, as the Christian church was just emerging, a disciple named Philip encountered an Ethiopian official puzzling over the words of Isaiah's lyrical prophecy. Philip used the words of Isaiah to explain the hope of salvation available through Jesus, the Lamb of God who came to take away the sins of anyone who would believe in him. The ancient prophecy became the catalyst by which the official heard and embraced the significance of Jesus' life and death (Acts 8:31–35).

The Crowining with Thorns, 1602–04 or 1607
Caravaggio (1573–1610)

REJECTED KING

Perhaps the cruelest irony of Jesus' death was that he became, in the words of the psalmist, "the stone that the builders tossed aside" (Psalm 118:22a). The New Testament quotes Psalm 118 no fewer than five times to highlight Jesus' painful rejection (Matthew 21:42; Mark 12:10; Luke 20:17; Acts 4:11; 1 Peter 2:7).

But the full quote reveals a double irony: While rejected by those he came to save, Jesus was accepted by God. To quote the psalmist, Jesus became "the most important stone"—the cornerstone of God's spiritual house, the church, which is made up of all Jesus' followers (Psalm 118:22b; see also 1 Peter 2:4–7).

But Jesus' suffering went beyond rejection; he was tortured and mocked as well. The Gospels describe how Jesus was spit upon, blindfolded, and beaten (Matthew 26:67–68; Mark 14:65; Luke 22:63–65)—a tragic and brutal picture that several Old Testament passages anticipate. And quotes from the Psalms indicate that Jesus' followers looked beyond the traditional books of prophecy to find foreshadowings of Jesus as a suffering Messiah.

The Gospels describe in detail how these visions were fulfilled: Roman officials mocked Jesus, clothing him in a purple robe (a sign of royalty), putting a twisted crown of thorns on his head, placing a wooden staff (a "reed") in his right hand, and sarcastically calling him the "King of the Jews." And just as the prophets foretold, they struck him in the face before leading him to his death (Isaiah 50:6; Micah 5:1; Matthew 27:27–30).

94

Matthew 27:27–30

The governor's soldiers led Jesus into the fortress and brought together the rest of the troops. They stripped off Jesus' clothes and put a scarlet robe on him. They made a crown of thorn branches and placed it on his head, and they put a stick in his right hand. The soldiers knelt down and pretended to worship him. They made fun of him and shouted, "Hey, you king of the Jews!" Then they spit on him. They took the stick from him and beat him on the head with it.

1 Peter 2:4–7

(See also Matthew 21:42; Mark 12:10; Luke 20:17; Acts 4:11.)
Come to Jesus Christ. He is the living stone people have rejected, but which God has chosen and highly honored.

And now you are living stones that are being used to build a spiritual house. You are also a group of holy priests, and with the help of Jesus Christ you will offer sacrifices that please God. It is just as God says in the Scriptures,

"Look! I am placing in Zion a choice and precious cornerstone. No one who has faith in this one will be disappointed."

You are followers of the Lord, and this stone is precious to you. But it isn't precious to those who refuse to follow him. They are the builders who tossed aside the stone that turned out to be the most important one of all.

"THE STONE THAT THE BUILDERS TOSSED ASIDE HAS NOW BECOME THE MOST IMPORTANT STONE."
PSALM 118:22

Christ at the Column, c. 1476
Antonello Da Messina (c. 1430–79)

ISAIAH'S SUFFERING SERVANT

Jesus' followers understood the prophecy recorded in Isaiah 52:13–53:12 as perhaps the Old Testament's most poetic description of the Messiah's suffering on the cross. Isaiah gave specific details about the "servant's" emotional and physical experience—that the Messiah would be hated and rejected, his life filled with sorrow and terrible suffering.

According to the prophet, God's chosen servant would "endure great pain" after an "unfair trial." He would be "wounded and crushed," not as punishment from God, but because of humanity's sin.

The four Gospels describe Jesus' death as the complete fulfillment of Isaiah's prophecy. In all, Isaiah made more than twenty specific prophecies about the Messiah, all of which were fulfilled in the records of the life, death, and resurrection of Jesus.

In Luke 22:44 and 23:35 we see how Jesus endured great anguish, particularly when he prayed in the Garden of Gethsemane and when he was despised and rejected by those surrounding him while he was on the cross. According to the New Testament writers, Jesus carried more than the physical burden of the cross on his back; he also carried the burden of humanity's sin (1 Peter 2:24). One of the most striking aspects of the suffering of Jesus is that, even though he suffered for all humanity, he did so in silence (Matthew 27:12; 1 Peter 2:22–23).

Isaiah's image of the Messiah as the suffering servant is reflected in some of the letters written to the earliest Christians (Romans 3:25; 6:9–10; 1 Corinthians 15:3–4; Philippians 2:6–11; Hebrews 9:28). Christian tradition points to the words of the prophet as best explaining the significance of Jesus' suffering on the cross:

*By suffering, the servant
will learn the true meaning
of obeying the LORD.
Although he is innocent,
he will take the punishment
for the sins of others,
so that many of them
will no longer be guilty.
The LORD will reward him
with honor and power
for sacrificing his life.
Others thought he was a sinner,
but he suffered for our sins
and asked God to forgive us.*
(Isaiah 53:11–12)

Agony in the Garden
Andrea Mantegna
c.1460

■ **Isaiah 53:2b–8a, 10a**

He wasn't some handsome king. Nothing about the way he looked made him attractive to us.

He was hated and rejected; his life was filled with sorrow and terrible suffering. No one wanted to look at him. We despised him and said, "He is a nobody!" He suffered and endured great pain for us, but we thought his suffering was punishment from God. He was wounded and crushed because of our sins; by taking our punishment, he made us completely well.

All of us were like sheep that had wandered off. We had each gone our own way, but the LORD gave him the punishment we deserved.

He was painfully abused, but he did not complain. He was silent like a lamb being led to the butcher, as quiet as a sheep having its wool cut off.

He was condemned to death without a fair trial. Who could have imagined what would happen to him?

. . .

The LORD decided his servant would suffer as a sacrifice to take away the sin and guilt of others.

Most people are probably acquainted with images of the suffering Jesus. Nearly everyone has seen an icon, a sculpture, or a painting of the wounded, dying Jesus, pierced through his hands and feet. Yet the effect of powerfully moving images such as these can be easily lost by their very familiarity. They can become separated from the gruesome reality of Jesus' physical suffering.

Crucifixion, because it involved both slow suffocation and loss of blood, was a brutal way to die, and Jesus endured excruciating agony. Again, the prophecies associated with Jesus' physical suffering are remarkably specific, yet he fulfilled each of them.

Several of the psalms alluded to the thirst Jesus would experience on the cross and even hinted at the soured wine or vinegar the executioners offered Jesus to quench his parched mouth (Psalms 22:15; 69:21). Both details are recounted most vividly in John's Gospel (John 19:28–29).

The Old Testament provides yet another insight into Jesus' suffering. Zechariah wrote of a Messiah who would be pierced with a spear and mourned over as parents mourn the death of a firstborn child. Exodus and Numbers both stated that the Passover lamb, a symbol of the messianic deliverer, would not have any of its bones broken. According

to John's Gospel, Jesus met this requirement—despite his violent death, none of his bones were broken (John 19:32–36).

■ **John 19:31–37**
The next day would be both a Sabbath and the Passover. It was a special day for the Jewish people, and they did not want the bodies to stay on the crosses during that day. So they asked Pilate to break the men's legs and take their bodies down. The soldiers first broke the legs of the other two men who were nailed there. But when they came to Jesus, they saw that he was already dead, and they did not break his legs. One of the soldiers stuck his spear into Jesus' side, and blood and water came out. We know this is true, because it was told by someone who saw it happen. Now you can have faith too. All this happened so that the Scriptures would come true, which say, "No bone of his body will be broken" and, "They will see the one in whose side they stuck a spear."

"ENEMIES POISONED MY FOOD, AND WHEN I WAS THIRSTY, THEY GAVE ME VINEGAR."
PSALM 69:21

MICAH

While many of the prophets of the Old Testament carried on their ministry in either the northern kingdom of Israel or the southern kingdom of Judah, the prophet Micah carried his message of judgment and restoration to both sides of the divided kingdom.

Micah's prophecy, which is made up of a series of oracles, includes a description of God's future king that includes his birthplace—Bethlehem. For many, of course, this draws a direct correlation between the king of Micah's prophecy and the birth of Jesus described in Matthew 2:1–6.

HIS SUFFERING BODY

> I, THE LORD, WILL MAKE THE DESCENDANTS OF DAVID AND THE PEOPLE OF JERUSALEM FEEL DEEP SORROW AND PRAY WHEN THEY SEE THE ONE THEY PIERCED WITH A SPEAR. THEY WILL MOURN AND WEEP FOR HIM, AS PARENTS WEEP OVER THE DEATH OF THEIR ONLY CHILD OR THEIR FIRST-BORN.
>
> ZECHARIAH 12:10

The Small Crucifixion, c. 1511–20
Matthias Grünewald (c. 1470–1528)

AFTER THE SOLDIERS HAD NAILED JESUS TO THE CROSS, THEY DIVIDED UP HIS CLOTHES INTO FOUR PARTS, ONE FOR EACH OF THEM. BUT HIS OUTER GARMENT WAS MADE FROM A SINGLE PIECE OF CLOTH, AND IT DID NOT HAVE ANY SEAMS.

THE SOLDIERS SAID TO EACH OTHER, "LET'S NOT RIP IT APART. WE WILL GAMBLE TO SEE WHO GETS IT." THIS HAPPENED SO THAT THE SCRIPTURES WOULD COME TRUE, WHICH SAY:

"THEY DIVIDED UP MY CLOTHES AND GAMBLED FOR MY GARMENTS."

THE SOLDIERS THEN DID WHAT THEY HAD DECIDED. JOHN 19:23–24

Psalm 22 echoes the abandonment Jesus experienced, and Jesus actually quoted the beginning of this psalm while hanging on the cross: *"My God, my God, why have you deserted me?"* (Psalm 22:1; Matthew 27:46; Mark 15:34). In the same Old Testament passage we find a clue that Jesus' clothes would be divided among his enemies (Psalm 22:18; John 19:23-24). Elsewhere, the prophet Amos described a day when God would darken the earth at noon—something that occurred on the day of Jesus' crucifixion (Amos 8:9; see also Matthew 27:45; Mark 15:33; Luke 23:44–45).

Even the events surrounding the aftermath of Jesus' death were a fulfillment of prophecy. In the ancient world, respectable citizens were normally kept separate from criminals, even in death. Yet the Gospels tell us that Jesus was buried in a rich man's tomb after being crucified along with criminals, just as Isaiah said the Messiah would be (Isaiah 53:9; see also Matthew 27:57-60; Mark 15:42-46; Luke 23:50-53; John 19:38-42).

top: ***Christ Before Caiaphas***
Matthias Stom, Early 1630s

left: ***The Entombment of Christ***
Caravaggio, 1602-1604

HIS CRUCIFIXION

The Gospel writers saw Old Testament prophecies being fulfilled in many of the details of Jesus' crucifixion. We know from two of the Gospel writers, Matthew and Mark, that Jesus was crucified along with two criminals and forsaken by almost all of his followers—details anticipated by the prophet Zechariah (Zechariah 13:7; see Matthew 26:31; Mark 14:50). Luke's description of Jesus' words of forgiveness from the cross (Luke 23:34) was an allusion to the words of the prophet Isaiah (Isaiah 53:12b).

PSALM TWENTY-TWO

MY GOD, my God, why have you deserted me? Why are you so far away? Won't you listen to my groans and come to my rescue? I cry out day and night, but you don't answer, and I can never rest. Yet you are the holy God, ruling from your throne and praised by Israel. Our ancestors trusted you, and you rescued them. When they cried out for help, you saved them, and you did not let them down when they depended on you. But I am merely a worm, far less than human, and I am hated and rejected by people everywhere. Everyone who sees me makes fun and sneers. They shake their heads, and say, "Trust the LORD! If you are his favorite, let him protect you and keep you safe." You, LORD, brought me safely through birth, and you protected me when I was a baby at my mother's breast. From the day I was born, I have been in your care, and from the time of my birth, you have been my God. Don't stay far off when I am in trouble with no one to help me. Enemies are all around like a herd of wild bulls. Powerful bulls from Bashan are everywhere. My enemies are like lions roaring and attacking with jaws open wide. I have no more strength than a few drops of water. All my bones are out of joint; my heart is like melted wax. My strength has dried up like a broken clay pot, and my tongue sticks to the roof of my mouth. You, God, have left me to die in the dirt. Brutal enemies attack me like a pack of dogs, tearing at my hands and my feet. I can count all my bones, and my enemies just stare and sneer at me. They took my clothes and gambled for them. Don't stay far away, LORD! My strength comes from you, so hurry and help. Rescue me from enemy swords and save me from those dogs. Don't let lions eat me. You rescued me from the horns of wild bulls, and when your people meet, I will praise you, LORD. All who worship the LORD, now praise him! You belong to Jacob's family and to the people of Israel, so fear and honor the LORD! The LORD doesn't hate or despise the helpless in all of their troubles. When I cried out, he listened and did not turn away. When your people meet, you will fill my heart with your praises, LORD, and everyone will see me keep my promises to you. The poor will eat and be full, and all who worship you will be thankful and live in hope. Everyone on this earth will remember you, LORD. People all over the world will turn and worship you, because you are in control, the ruler of all nations. All who are rich and have more than enough will bow down to you, Lord. Even those who are dying and almost in the grave will come and bow down. In the future, everyone will worship and learn about you, our Lord. People not yet born will be told, "The Lord has saved us!"

No detail of Jesus' story is more revolutionary than his resurrection. Although, looking back through time, it is possible to uncover foreshadowings of this event in the Old Testament scriptures, Jesus' triumph over the grave astounded even those closest to him.

The idea that death could be defeated is first introduced in the Old Testament account of the Garden of Eden (Genesis 3:15). Adam and Even chose their own way, defying God's command, and thus were expelled from paradise. God explained to each of them, and to the serpent who tempted them, that the eventual consequences of their choices would include death. But also included was a cryptic prophecy that a descendant of Adam and Eve would make right what had gone so terribly wrong. The sin of Adam—and its consequences—would be undone by a kind of second Adam who would restore the broken bond between God and his people (see Romans 5:12–21; 1 Corinthians 15:20–22). This is not to say that Jesus and Adam were equal opposites, only that understanding the significance of Adam's fall sheds light on the significance of Jesus' sacrifice.

The story of Jonah provides another allusion to the Messiah's death and resurrection. Just as Jonah spent three days in the belly of a large fish, Jesus spent three days in the grave. Likewise, Jonah's deliverance from the fish mirrors Jesus' resurrection from the grave (see Jonah 1:17).

Elsewhere, both the psalmist and the prophet Isaiah claimed God would not let his chosen one remain in death's grip. Instead, God would raise him from the grave and restore him to a position of honor at God's right hand (Psalm 16:10–11; Isaiah 53:11–12).

Stone of Unction inside Holy Sepulchre

Church of the Holy Sepulchre in the Old City of Jerusalem

■ Romans 5:12–21
Adam sinned, and that sin brought death into the world. Now everyone has sinned, and so everyone must die. Sin was in the world before the Law came. But no record of sin was kept, because there was no Law. Yet death still had power over all who lived from the time of Adam to the time of Moses. This happened, though not everyone disobeyed a direct command from God, as Adam did.

In some ways Adam is like Christ who came later. But the gift of God's undeserved grace was kind enough to give was very different from Adam's sin. That one sin brought death to many others. Yet in an even greater way, Jesus Christ alone brought God's gift of undeserved grace to many people.

There is a lot of difference between Adam's sin and God's gift. That one sin led to punishment. But God's gift made it possible for us to be acceptable to him, even though we have sinned many times. Death ruled like a king because Adam had sinned. But that cannot compare with what Jesus Christ has done. God has treated us with undeserved grace, and he has accepted us because of Jesus. And so we will live and rule like kings.

Everyone was going to be punished because Adam sinned. But because of the good thing that Christ has done, God accepts us and gives us the gift of life. Adam disobeyed God and caused many others to be sinners. But Jesus obeyed him and will make many people acceptable to God.

The Law came, so that the full power of sin could be seen. Yet where sin was powerful, God's gift of undeserved grace was even more powerful. Sin ruled by means of death. But God's gift of grace now rules, and God has accepted us because of Jesus Christ our Lord. This means that we will have eternal life.

HIS RESURRECTION

I AM YOUR CHOSEN ONE. YOU WON'T LEAVE ME IN THE GRAVE OR LET MY BODY DECAY. YOU HAVE SHOWN ME THE PATH TO LIFE, AND YOU MAKE ME GLAD BY BEING NEAR TO ME. SITTING AT YOUR RIGHT SIDE, I WILL ALWAYS BE JOYFUL.

PSALM 16:10–11

YOU HAVE BEEN RAISED TO LIFE WITH CHRIST. NOW SET YOUR HEART ON WHAT IS IN HEAVEN, WHERE CHRIST RULES AT GOD'S RIGHT SIDE. COLOSSIANS 3:1

Tapestry detail from the Vatican Museum showing the resurrection of Jesus Christ

Miniature from Rabbula Gospels
Mesopotamia, 6th century

RETURN TO GLORY

One last important detail follows the stories of Jesus' death and resurrection: He was restored to his glory as the Son of God. Jesus shared our humanity and thus understands our personal struggles as imperfect people. But according to the New Testament, he was not only a man; he was God's Son.

The prophecies about the Messiah's glory built tremendous expectation in the hearts of ancient Israelites. The Messiah was the one person who, according to God's promise, would bring victory to the nation and right all wrongs done to its people (Psalms 60:5; 98:1–3; Isaiah 40:9–10; 51:4–8).

Various Old Testament passages described not only how Jesus would rejoin God at a position of honor (Psalm 110:1), but also how Jesus would become the foundation for God's people—the cornerstone (Psalm 118:22–23; Isaiah 28:16). Centuries later, the New Testament writers described how Jesus ascended into heaven, where he was restored to glory and seated at the right hand of God (Acts 1:1–11; Romans 8:34; Ephesians 1:19–23; Colossians 3:1).

■ Ephesians 1:19–23

I want you to know about the great and mighty power that God has for us followers. It is the same wonderful power he used when he raised Christ from death and let him sit at his right side in heaven. There Christ rules over all forces, authorities, powers, and rulers. He rules over all beings in this world and will rule in the future world as well. God has put all things under the power of Christ, and for the good of the church he has made him the head of everything. The church is Christ's body and is filled with Christ who completely fills everything.

■ Psalm 98:1–3

Sing a new song to the LORD!
He has worked miracles,
and with his own powerful arm,
he has won the victory.
The LORD has shown the nations
that he has the power to save
and to bring justice.
God has been faithful
in his love for Israel,
and his saving power is seen
everywhere on earth.

The Empty Throne (Second Coming of Christ).
6th century AD. Early Christian

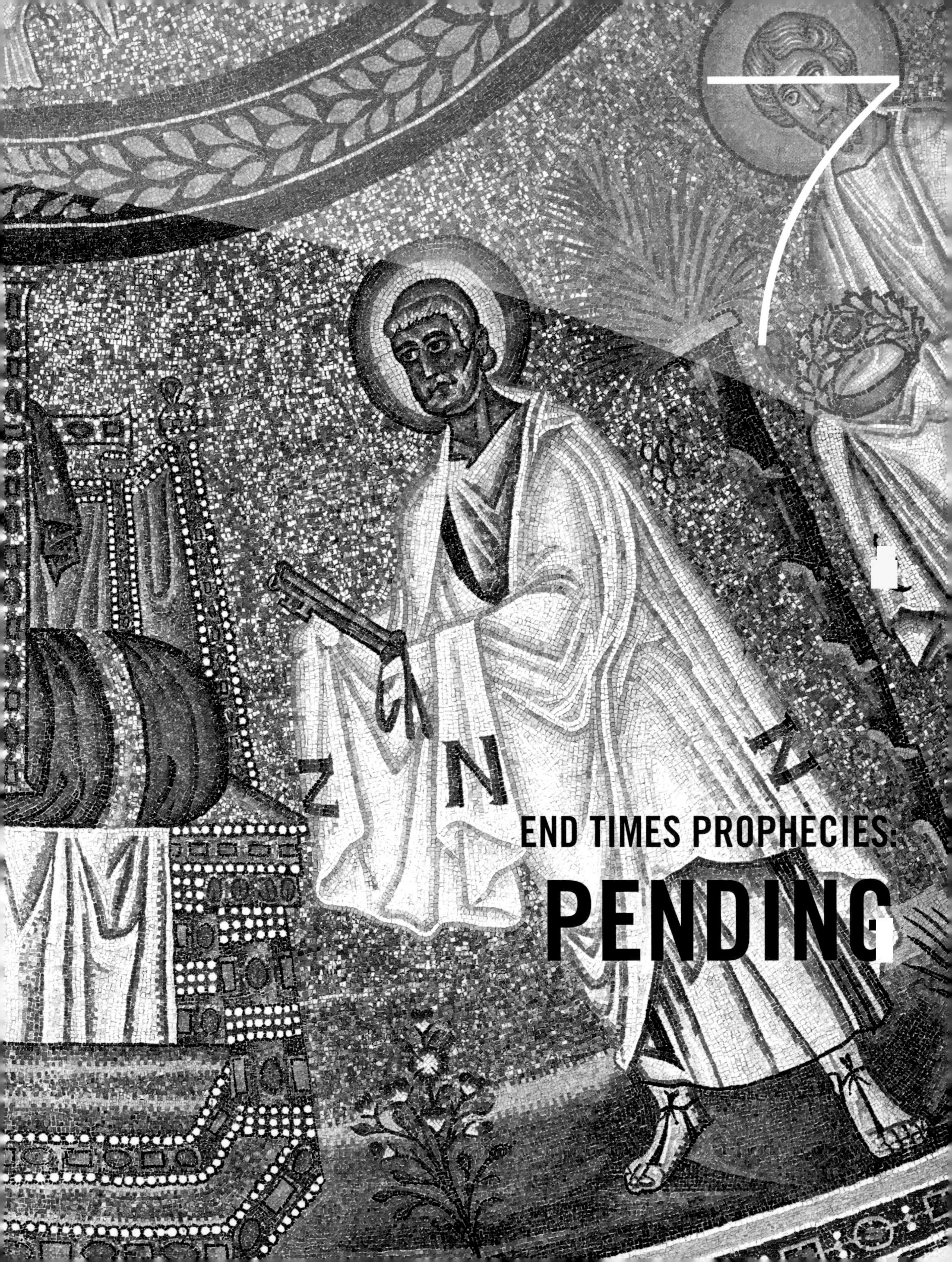

END TIMES PROPHECIES:

PENDING

7

OUR UNDERSTANDINGS OF JESUS' RETURN TO EARTH, CALLED THE SECOND COMING—AND THE OFTEN-STUDIED AND MUCH-DEBATED "END-TIMES" EVENTS THAT SURROUND IT— ARE ROOTED IN THE PROPHECIES OF THE BIBLE.

To the first-century men and women who read the writings of the New Testament while they were being circulated as individual letters, Jesus' promise to return carried with it the hope that justice would be done and faith rewarded.

That hope still resonates in our world. While images of angels descending, triumphal trumpets being sounded, and people standing before great white thrones may seem strange to our contemporary Western culture, the message behind those images is clear: Someone trustworthy will make the final judgment on right and wrong, and in the end, one's faith— or lack of faith—will make a difference.

JESUS SAID TO HIS DISCIPLES, "DON'T BE WORRIED! HAVE FAITH IN GOD AND HAVE FAITH IN ME. THERE ARE MANY ROOMS IN MY FATHER'S HOUSE. I WOULDN'T TELL YOU THIS, UNLESS IT WAS TRUE. I AM GOING THERE TO PREPARE A PLACE FOR EACH OF YOU. AFTER I HAVE DONE THIS, I WILL COME BACK AND TAKE YOU WITH ME. THEN WE WILL BE TOGETHER."

JOHN 14:1–3

LIKE A THIEF
in the Night

The pages of the New Testament ring with hope—the unshakable conviction that Jesus will return for his followers. In his letter to Titus, the apostle Paul encouraged the church leader to continue living a "decent and honest" life until Jesus' return (Titus 2:12–13). But for Paul, the return of Jesus was not just some faraway event; it was something on which he hinged his expectations .

Many of the prophecies about Jesus' return can be found in his own teachings. Matthew's Gospel records a conversation between Jesus and his disciples on the Mount of Olives, during which Jesus revealed what the disciples could expect in the future. The events described by Jesus would culminate in his return: *"And there will be the Son of Man. All nations on earth will weep when they see the Son of Man coming on the clouds of heaven with power and great glory"* (Matthew 24:30; see also Mark 13:21–27; Luke 21:25–28).

While Jesus described the signs that would accompany his return, he was swift to emphasize that the timing would be impossible to forecast. Jesus said no one could know the time of his return, not even the angels—not even Jesus himself. Only God knows when it will take place (Matthew 24:36).

Years later, when writing a letter to Christians in Thessalonica (a region of modern-day Greece), the apostle Paul expected that Christ would return during the lifetime of his readers (1 Thessalonians 4:13–18). But in his next letter to the same church, Paul modified this apocalyptic expectation by saying that a series of historical events would have to take place first before Christ returns (2 Thessalonians 2:1–12). Paul compared the return of Christ to a nighttime thief arriving when no one expects him (1 Thessalonians 5:1–2)—the implication being that Jesus' followers should live in a state of constant preparation and anticipation, knowing that day may come at any time (1 Thessalonians 5:4–8). Despite this, many people continue to speculate on the date of Jesus' return.

Even if the timing cannot be known, Jesus made clear that no one would be able to miss the event itself. Prophesying from the Mount of Olives, Jesus explained that his return would be visible to all no matter what their faith (Matthew 24:27).

Luke, the author of the Gospel that bears his name as well as the book of Acts, documented Jesus' ascension into heaven. As the disciples watched his ascent, two men appeared and told them that Jesus would return in the same way he left—in person, in plain sight, on the clouds of heaven (Acts 1:11).

While there is much to debate concerning the details of Jesus' return, many believe it will set into motion other events, such as the taking up of Christians to heaven (sometimes called "the rapture"), the overpowering of evil (Revelation 20:1–3), an extended period in which Jesus would rule on earth (Revelation 20:4–6), and the restoration of the nation of Israel (Acts 15:16–18). The Hebrew and early Christian prophetic and apocalyptic writings were thus self-correcting and fluid.

SUFFERING
and Survival

The book of Acts paints a portrait of people gathered together for teaching, community, and worship (Acts 2:42–47). This is the church—followers of Jesus committed to experiencing and sharing the good news. *Church* is a term that refers both to the global body of Christians as well as to individual congregations of people gathered for worship. The early church grew quickly as news about Jesus spread.

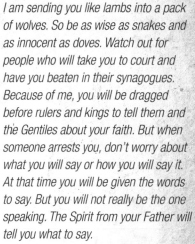

With this growth came recognition—a visibility that sometimes resulted in persecution and suffering. But the Christian church has endured. Both the suffering and the survival of the church were prophesied in scripture.

During his time on earth, Jesus talked about the persecution and struggles his followers could expect. They would be hated, Jesus warned (John 15:18). He also promised that those who remained faithful would survive (Matthew 10:22). Jesus was persecuted and killed because of his teaching, and he told his followers to prepare for the same treatment. Amazingly, however, he said that this was not to be a cause for discouragement. Instead, Jesus taught that persecution for doing what is right is a part of what it means to be faithful, and faithful endurance is something God promises to reward (Matthew 5:10–12).

Jesus spoke these prophecies prior to his own suffering and death. They proved true almost immediately after the church was born. As a result of persecution, Jesus' first followers in Jerusalem scattered throughout the region (see Acts 5:17–42; 8:1). It seems that, as recorded throughout the book of Acts, the church grew in proportion to its suffering.

Today, Christians in some parts of the world continue to face persecution because of their beliefs, which some would argue indicates the ongoing fulfillment of Jesus' prophecy. But Jesus' followers take heart when they remember his words to the disciple Simon Peter: Even death, Jesus promised, would not overpower the church (Matthew 16:18). John's apocalyptic book, called Revelation, describes both the church's endurance until the very end of days and the rewards for those who withstand persecution (Revelation 3:8–11; 7:9–17).

MATTHEW 10:16–22

I am sending you like lambs into a pack of wolves. So be as wise as snakes and as innocent as doves. Watch out for people who will take you to court and have you beaten in their synagogues. Because of me, you will be dragged before rulers and kings to tell them and the Gentiles about your faith. But when someone arrests you, don't worry about what you will say or how you will say it. At that time you will be given the words to say. But you will not really be the one speaking. The Spirit from your Father will tell you what to say.

Brothers and sisters will betray one another and have each other put to death. Parents will betray their own children, and children will turn against their parents and have them killed. Everyone will hate you because of me. But if you remain faithful until the end, you will be saved.

Photos on right page courtesy of Strategic World Impact

MARK 13:19–23
*This will be the worst time of
suffering since God created the world,
and nothing this terrible will ever
happen again. If the Lord doesn't
make the time shorter, no one will be
left alive. But because of his chosen
and special ones, he will make the
time shorter.*

ANTICHRIST
Man in the Shadows

Persecution is not the only threat to the church, according to the Bible. Jesus warned his followers that false messiahs and prophets would try to fool God's people by working miracles and signs (Matthew 24:4-5, 23-24; see also Mark 13:5-6, 21-22).

They would claim to teach God's truth, but would in fact lead the people away from the truth. The Bible has a word for people like this: antichrist—literally, "false messiah."

Many believe that Jesus' warning is not the Bible's first reference to an antichrist. The Old Testament book of Daniel mentions a ruler who would come and persecute the people of God (Daniel 7:25). Some claim the prophecy was fulfilled when the Greek ruler Antiochus IV Epiphanes came to power (175–164 BC) and brutally oppressed the Jewish people. Others agree that the prophecy was immediately fulfilled in Antiochus's rise to power, but suggest that ultimately this prophecy will be fulfilled in the person referred to later as the antichrist.

In his second letter to the church at Thessalonica (in an important adjustment to what he wrote in his first letter to the Thessalonians), Paul describes in detail someone called "the wicked one," which may be taken to be a reference to the antichrist. He will bring destruction; he will be boastful; he will oppose everything that is holy. He will sit in God's temple, claim to be God, and fool people into following him instead of Jesus (2 Thessalonians 2:1–12). But Paul goes on to prophesy that the antichrist will be no match for Jesus, who "will kill him simply by breathing on him" (2 Thessalonians 2:8). In short, the antichrist doesn't stand a chance.

Revelation, an apocalyptic vision of the end times and final judgment, describes a beast from the sea with characteristics similar to those of the "wicked one" mentioned in 2 Thessalonians. This leads many to identify John's beast as the antichrist (Revelation 13:1-10). If this is the case, the prophecy about the antichrist may be one that is yet to be completely fulfilled.

In two New Testament letters we read that some false prophets had already begun to appear in the late first century (1 John 2:18). These letters offer two rather straightforward markers for identifying false prophets:
- They deny that Jesus is the Son of God (1 John 2:18–27).
- They deny Jesus' true humanity (1 John 4:1–3; 2 John 7).

DANIEL

The prophecies of Daniel, though quite symbolic in nature, are associated with the end of the age and Jesus' return.

Daniel's life as a prophet was unusual. He was one of the young men of Judah who were carried away into exile in Babylonia. As was the custom of the day, when a country was overtaken, the best and strongest were taken captive for two reasons: first, to lessen the chances of, in this case, a Judean uprising, and second, to bolster the resources of Babylonia, the conquering country.

The opening of the Old Testament book attributed to Daniel offers several accounts of Daniel and his friends ingeniously surviving their capture and standing for their faith. These accounts offer insight into Daniel's rise to power even in a foreign culture, including his ability to interpret dreams.

A Great
TRIBULATION

Surviving a night in a lion's den was enough to make the Old Testament prophet Daniel famous, but he was also highly regarded as an interpreter of dreams, a channel for prophetic messages from God. Many of these prophecies may refer to future events related to the final days before God completes his work in the world.

REVELATION 7:13–17

One of the elders asked me, "Do you know who these people are that are dressed in white robes? Do you know where they come from?"

"Sir," I answered, "you must know." Then he told me: "These are the ones who have gone through the great suffering. They have washed their robes in the blood of the Lamb and have made them white. And so they stand before the throne of God and worship him in his temple day and night. The one who sits on the throne will spread his tent over them.

They will never hunger or thirst again, and they won't be troubled by the sun or any scorching heat. The Lamb in the center of the throne will be their shepherd. He will lead them to streams of life-giving water, and God will wipe all tears from their eyes."

While Daniel envisioned a glorious end, complete with God's absolute victory over evil and the restoration of a perfect world, this happy ending will not come easily, he counseled (see Daniel 12; Matthew 25; Revelation 20–22).

The seer and prophet Daniel warns of suffering and destruction that must take place before God's work is complete (Daniel 9:20–27). These apocalyptic sayings are often referred to as "The Seventy Weeks" because they hint at seventy weeks of suffering to be experienced by the Israelites. According to the messenger in Daniel's dreams, the suffering is a punishment that will usher in the disappearance of evil and the rule of justice (Daniel 9:24). Biblical scholars interpret the description of Seventy Weeks in different ways. It is unclear whether the weeks are literal or figurative—much less how many of them have already taken place. But Daniel indicates the suffering will increase until the archangel Michael comes to protect God's children from the world around them (Daniel 12:1).

In words reminiscent of Daniel, Jesus warned his followers that they would experience a time of suffering never seen before and never to be seen again (Mark 13:19). Some interpreters

think this refers to Daniel's prophecy of the final "week" (Daniel 9:27) and the tribulation described in Revelation—a time of suffering for Christians prior to Jesus' return (Matthew 24:15–22; Revelation 7:13–17). Others believe that Christians will be spared this. John's apocalyptic vision in Revelation described this period of suffering in vivid detail (Revelation 6–19).

JUSTICE & JUDGMENT

The Bible represents God as just. Justice demands accountability—that is, judgment. The Old Testament prophets anticipated a final day of judgment. They called it by different names—"that terrible day" (Zephaniah 1:14), "the day . . . will be like a red-hot furnace, with flames that burn up proud and sinful people, as though they were straw" (Malachi 4:1), or "the day when . . . all will be darkness" (Amos 5:18). Their prophecies describe judgment as a day of reckoning for all the nations of the world, as well as for individuals who will be held accountable for the way they lived their lives (Isaiah 3:10–11).

In the New Testament, the teachings of the prophets merge seamlessly

with Jesus' teachings. The Son of Man, Jesus told his disciples, would come to sit on his throne and separate the nations like sheep and goats—sheep on his right and goats on his left. The sheep would be those who are blessed because of the way they lived. The goats would be those who receive judgment (Matthew 25:31-46).

John's apocalyptic drama in Revelation provides yet more detail about this final day of reckoning, describing how Jesus will judge the wicked and the righteous after his return. According to John's prophecy, it is at this final judgment that Jesus will destroy death and evil forever—and that the salvation of the righteous will be complete (Revelation 20).

While the Bible presents the judgment of God as inevitable, it also offers certain hope of rescue from that judgment. Jesus' disciple Peter wrote, *"Put all your hope in how God will treat you with undeserved grace when Jesus Christ appears"* (1 Peter 1:13).

As John's apocalyptic drama unfolds in Revelation, the great judgment day is followed by the creation of a new heaven and a new earth, where God's people live with him forever. *"God's home is now with his people. He will live with them, and they will be his own. Yes, God will make his home among his people. He will wipe all tears from their eyes, and there will be no more death, suffering, crying, or pain. These things of the past are gone forever"* (Revelation 21:3-4).

REVELATION 20:11–21:5

I saw a great white throne with someone sitting on it. Earth and heaven tried to run away, but there was no place for them to go. I also saw all the dead people standing in front of that throne. Every one of them was there, no matter who they had once been. Several books were opened, and then the book of life was opened. The dead were judged by what those books said they had done. The sea gave up the dead people who were in it, and death and its kingdom also gave up their dead. Then everyone was judged by what they had done. Afterwards, death and its kingdom were thrown into the lake of fire. This is the second death. Anyone whose name wasn't written in the book of life was thrown into the lake of fire.
....

I heard a loud voice shout from the throne: God's home is now with his people. He will live with them, and they will be his own. Yes, God will make his home among his people. He will wipe all tears from their eyes, and there will be no more death, suffering, crying, or pain. These things of the past are gone forever.

Then the one sitting on the throne said: "I am making everything new. Write down what I have said. My words are true and can be trusted."

far left:
Angel of the Revelation
ca.1803–1805, William Blake

immediate left:
Vision of St. John the Evangelist on Patmos
Alberegno, Jacobello (d.1397)

EPILOGUE

FULFILLMENT OF THE PROMISES

READING ABOUT PROPHECY THAT HAS BEEN FULFILLED CAN BE FASCINATING. BUT MANY FIND HOPE AND INSPIRATION IN THE PROPHECIES THAT HAVE BEEN ISSUED BUT ARE YET TO BE FULFILLED.

In some ways, Christ's followers today find themselves in a similar position to the members of the early church. They have received the same promises as the ones we read in the New Testament—promises that Jesus would come again and justice would be done once and for all. As far as those first believers knew, the fulfillment of these promises was just around the corner. Yet nearly two thousand years have passed, and we are still waiting to see how events will unfold.

The prophecies of the Bible are discussed and debated today, much as they might have been in the early days of the church. But whether one regards these passages as symbolic or literal, it's important to recall that there seemed to be a greater issue weighing on the minds of the prophets themselves—that is, how people choose to live their lives as they wait for the prophecies to be fulfilled.

If a new world is coming and everyone will be held accountable for the way they lived, the ultimate question the prophets would have us ask is: In what manner are we living? Are we looking ahead eagerly?

Do we have confidence that we are prepared for whatever the future holds? Are we living a life of patient service and joyful proclamation as we wait?

Biblical prophecy, by its very nature, assumes there is a place outside of time and a divine being not bound by the unfolding of human history. The past, present, and future are connected. The amazing thing about prophecy is not so much that it predicts the future; it is the idea that it connects our world—the days, weeks, months, years, and the events that fill them—with a place and a God who is bigger than time.

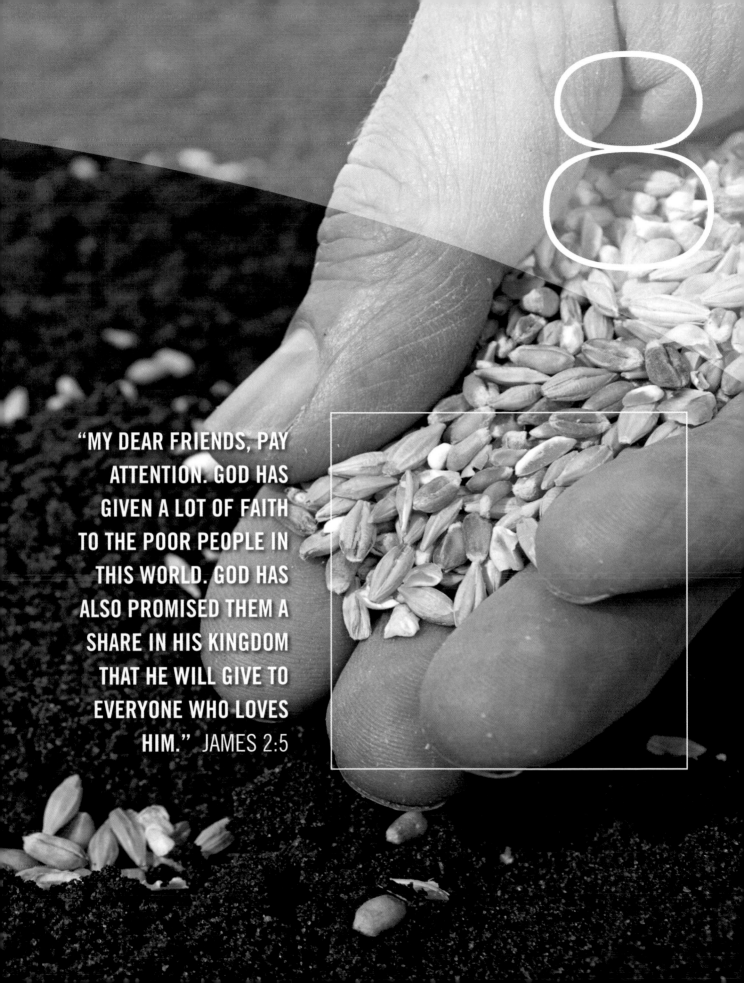

"MY DEAR FRIENDS, PAY ATTENTION. GOD HAS GIVEN A LOT OF FAITH TO THE POOR PEOPLE IN THIS WORLD. GOD HAS ALSO PROMISED THEM A SHARE IN HIS KINGDOM THAT HE WILL GIVE TO EVERYONE WHO LOVES HIM." JAMES 2:5

8

ON THE EDGE OF OUR SEATS

If nothing else, the prophecies of the Bible offer hope, the idea that we can expect something else from our lives, something better. Many of those who first read the New Testament's prophecies of Jesus' return were facing persecution for their faith. The end must have seemed close on the horizon. This hope enabled them to anticipate a future where justice and mercy would triumph, no matter how bad things seemed at the time.

These same prophecies can offer hope to our world as well. In the face of uncertainty, injustice, and oppression, we are still offered a hope that this life extends beyond what we can see and that someday the scales will be balanced. In a world so often filled with injustice, this expectation is more than welcome.

JESUS SAID, I CAME SO EVERYONE WOULD HAVE LIFE, AND HAVE IT FULLY.

JOHN 10:10

2 PETER 3:10–14

■ **THE DAY OF THE LORD'S RETURN WILL SURPRISE US LIKE A THIEF. THE HEAVENS WILL DISAPPEAR WITH A LOUD NOISE, AND THE HEAT WILL MELT THE WHOLE UNIVERSE.** THEN THE EARTH AND EVERYTHING ON IT WILL BE SEEN FOR WHAT THEY ARE. EVERYTHING WILL BE DESTROYED. SO YOU SHOULD SERVE AND HONOR GOD BY THE WAY YOU LIVE. YOU SHOULD LOOK FORWARD TO THE DAY WHEN GOD JUDGES EVERYONE, AND YOU SHOULD TRY TO MAKE IT COME SOON. ON THAT DAY THE HEAVENS WILL BE DESTROYED BY FIRE, AND EVERYTHING ELSE WILL MELT IN THE HEAT. BUT GOD HAS PROMISED US A NEW HEAVEN AND A NEW EARTH, WHERE JUSTICE WILL RULE. WE ARE REALLY LOOKING FORWARD TO THIS! MY FRIENDS, WHILE YOU ARE WAITING, YOU SHOULD MAKE CERTAIN THE LORD FINDS YOU PURE, SPOTLESS, AND LIVING AT PEACE.

TITUS 2:11–14

God has shown us undeserved grace by coming to save all people. He taught us to give up our wicked ways and our worldly desires and to live decent and honest lives in this world. We are filled with hope, as we wait for the glorious return of our great God and Savior Jesus Christ. He gave himself to rescue us from everything evil and to make our hearts pure. He wanted us to be his own people and to be eager to do right.

LONGING FOR WHAT'S AHEAD

The apostle Paul, writer of many of the New Testament letters, told his readers that faith involved a change of citizenship. Christ's followers were no longer citizens of this world only, but "citizens of heaven" as well (Ephesians 2:19–22; Philippians 3:20–21). It is only natural that a citizen of heaven would long for a bit of paradise.

Yet faith is not meant to be a form of frantic escapism that keeps us from living meaningfully in the present. Paul warned against this kind of response to prophecy when he admonished Christians in Thessalonica to "settle down and start working for a living" (2 Thessalonians 3:12). Taken as a whole, the Bible describes God's people as those who live fully in the here and now—the abundant life offered by Jesus—and at the same time hope for the future promises still to come.

ROMANS 8:23–25

The Spirit makes us sure about what we will be in the future. But now we groan silently, while we wait for God to show that we are his children. This means that our bodies will also be set free. And this hope is what saves us. But if we already have what we hope for, there is no need to keep on hoping. However, we hope for something we have not yet seen, and we patiently wait for it.

2 CORINTHIANS 5:1–5

Our bodies are like tents that we live in here on earth. But when these tents are destroyed, we know that God will give each of us a place to live. These homes will not be buildings someone has made, but they are in heaven and will last forever. While we are here on earth, we sigh because we want to live in that heavenly home. We want to put it on like clothes and not be naked.

These tents we now live in are like a heavy burden, and we groan. But we don't do this just because we want to leave these bodies that will die. It is because we want to change them for bodies that will never die. God is the one who makes all this possible. He has given us his Spirit to make us certain he will do it.

PHILIPPIANS 4:4–8

Always be glad because of the Lord! I will say it again: Be glad. Always be gentle with others. The Lord will soon be here. Don't worry about anything, but pray about everything. With thankful hearts offer up your prayers and requests to God. Then, because you belong to Christ Jesus, God will bless you with peace that no one can completely understand. And this peace will control the way you think and feel.

Finally, my friends, keep your minds on whatever is true, pure, right, holy, friendly, and proper. Don't ever stop thinking about what is truly worthwhile and worthy of praise.

HEADS HELD HIGH

Though the prophecies of the Bible contain many elements of judgment, they are not meant to be a scare tactic to frighten people into faith. The prophets meant to inspire hope and confidence among those who listened for God's voice and acted in faith, even when that meant believing in something yet unseen.

The emphasis on judgment reveals the consequences of bad and selfish choices that cause us to disobey God, referred to as sin. It is a basic tenet that runs throughout scripture—humanity either chooses God's way and thrives, or chooses the wrong path and dies (see, for example, Deuteronomy 28).

From a biblical perspective, this is the purpose of Jesus' life, death, and resurrection. This is what the voices we hear in the Bible are telling us—both the prophets of the Old Testament who were addressing the nation of Israel and the writers of the New Testament who were interpreting these ancient prophecies for the members of Christ's early church. Both were offered the hope of restoration, the invitation to choose eternal life over death. And so is each of us today.

HEBREWS 10:21–23, 32–38a

We have a great high priest who is in charge of God's house. So let's come near God with pure hearts and a confidence that comes from having faith. Let's keep our hearts pure, our consciences free from evil, and our bodies washed with clean water. We must hold tightly to the hope we say is ours. After all, we can trust the one who made the agreement with us. . . .

Don't forget all the hard times you went through when you first received the light. Sometimes you were abused and mistreated in public, and at other times you shared in the sufferings of others. You were kind to people in jail. And you gladly let your possessions be taken away, because you knew you had something better, something that would last forever.

Keep on being brave! It will bring you great rewards. Learn to be patient, so you will please God and be given what he has promised. As the Scriptures say, "God is coming soon! It won't be very long." The people God accepts will live because of their faith.

SOURCES

EDITORIAL SOURCES

Prophecies of the Bible is not intended to be a definitive source of information; rather, it was written to invite you to explore for yourself the significance of the prophets of the Bible and their writings. As we compiled our research, we took great care to question and verify. Now, we offer you the opportunity to research and verify our findings as well, and we invite you to further explore these prophetic writings for yourself.

BOOKS

Bible Atlas & Companion.
David Barrett, Christopher D. Hudson, and Todd Bolen
Uhrichsville, Ohio:
Barbour Publishing, 2008.

The Theology of the Book of Revelation.
Richard Bauckham
Cambridge University Press, 1993.

Holman Illustrated Bible Dictionary.
Trent C. Butler, Chad-Brand, Charles Draper, Archie England, eds.
Nashville: B&H Publishing Group, 2003.

Tyndale Bible Dictionary.
Walter A. Elwell and Philip W. Comfort, eds. Wheaton, Ill.:
Tyndale House Publishers, 2008.

How to Read Prophecy.
Joel Green
Downers Grove, Ill.: InterVarsity Press, 1984.

The New Interpreter's Bible Commentary, 12 vols.
Leander E. Keck, and others, eds.
Nashville: Abingdon Press,
1994–1998.

Breaking the Code: Understanding the Book of Revelation.
Bruce Metzger
Nashville: Abingdon Press, 2006.

The Rapture Exposed: The Message of Hope in the Book of Revelation.
Barbara Rossing
New Y ork: Basic Books, 2005.

The Essential Bible Companion: Key Insights for Reading God's Word.
John H. Walton, Mark L. Strauss, and Ted Cooper Jr.
Grand Rapids, Mich.: Zondervan, 2006.

ONLINE SOURCES

100prophecies.org
aboutbibleprophecy.com
bible-prophecy.com
bibleprophecy.net
bibleprophecyfulfilled.org
bibleprophesy.org
en.wikipedia.org
fulfilledprophecy.com
soniclight.com

ART SOURCES

ART RESOURCE

Bronze coin of Herod I 'the Great', King of Judaea,
Jewish, 37–4 BCE
On this side (reverse) is a helmet with cheek pieces.
Wt: 9.687 g; Dia: 2.3 cm. CM 1908-1-10-263 (BMC Herod I 1).
Location: British Museum, London, Great Britain
Photo Credit: © The Trustees of The British Museum / Art
Resource, NY

Palace of King Herod the Great (37–4 BCE)
With Hellenistic tower, columnated courtyard, synagogue
(Synagogue 2nd BCE).
Location: Palace of King Herod the Great, Herodion, Israel
Photo Credit: Erich Lessing / Art Resource, NY

Abraham Sends Hagar Away, 1837
Vernet, Horace (1789–1863)
Location: Musee des Beaux-Arts, Nantes, France
Photo Credit: Erich Lessing / Art Resource, NY

Jehu, King of Israel, prostrating himself before
King Shalmaneser III of Assyria
Basalt bas-relief on the black stele of Shlamaneser III.
Assyrian, 9th BCE.
Location: British Museum, London, Great Britain
Photo Credit: Erich Lessing / Art Resource, NY

Christ Heals a Blind Man
Relief (3rd CE) on an early Christian sarcophagus
from Mezzocamino, Via Ostiense, Rome: Cat. 41.
Location: Museo Nazionale Romano (Terme di Diocleziano),
Museo Nazionale Romano, Rome, Italy
Photo Credit: Erich Lessing / Art Resource, NY

Nehemiah Looks Upon the Ruins of Jerusalem,
c. 1896–1902
Tissot, James Jacques Joseph (1836–1902)
Gouache on board.
Photo by John Parnell.
Location: The Jewish Museum, New York, NY, U.S.A.
Photo Credit: The Jewish Museum, NY / Art Resource, NY

The Seven Trumpets of Jericho, c.1896–1902
Tissot, James Jacques Joseph (1836–1902)
Gouache on board.
Photo by John Parnell.
Location: The Jewish Museum, New York, NY, U.S.A.
Photo Credit: The Jewish Museum, NY / Art Resource, NY

Jonah Thrown Overboard to the Whale
Brill, Paul (1554–1626)
Location: Ca' d'Oro, Venice, Italy
Photo Credit: Cameraphoto Arte, Venice / Art Resource, NY

The Palaces of Nimroud Restored
Baynes, Thomas Mann (1794–after 1854)
Location: British Library, London, Great Britain
Photo Credi : HIP / Art Resource, NY

Allegory, Apocalypse, Last Judgment, etc.,
oil on canvas, 1674
Heintz, Joseph the Younger (1600–1678)
Location: Kunsthistorisches Museum, Vienna, Austria
Photo Credit: Erich Lessing / Art Resource, NY

The Sacrifice of Abel and Melchizedek
(detail of Melchizedek)
Early Christian mosaic.
Location: S. Vitale, Ravenna, Italy
Photo Credit: Scala / Art Resource, NY

Scenes from the life of Jesus Christ: Payment of Judas,
15th century
Location: Chapelle St. Antoine, Bessans, France
Photo Credit: Scala / Art Resource, NY

The Empty Throne (Second Coming of Christ)
Detail from the mosaic of the Dome of the Baptistery
of the Arians.
6th CE. Early Christian.
Location: Baptistery of the Arians, Ravenna, Italy
Photo Credit: Scala/Ministero per i Beni e le Attività
culturali / Art Resource, NY

Vision of St. John the Evangelist on Patmos
Alberegno, Jacobello (d.1397)
Location: Accademia, Venice, Italy
Photo Credit: Cameraphoto / Art Resource, NY

Angel of the Revelation (Book of Revelation, chapter 10);
"And the Angel Which I Saw Lifted Up his Hand to Heaven".
ca.1803-1805.
Blake, William (1757–1827)
Location: The Metropolitan Museum of Art, New York, NY, U.S.A.
Photo Credit: Image copyright © The Metropolitan Museum
of Art / Art Resource, NY

The Last Judgment
Jordaens, Jacob (1593–1678)
Oil on canvas.
Photo: René-Gabriel Ojéda.
Location: Louvre Museum, Paris, France
Photo Credit: Réunion des Musées Nationaux /
Art Resource, NY

Ecce Homo, 1891
Ciseri, Antonio (1821–1891)
Oil on canvas.
Location: Galleria d'Arte Moderna, Florence, Italy
Photo Credit: Scala / Art Resource, NY

GETTY IMAGES

Man using telescope to view distant hills
Image no. 56903141
Royalty-free
Photographer: John Lund/Sam Diephuis

MISCELLANEOUS

120 Great Paintings of the Life of Christ
Dover Platinum Electronic Clip Art

Bible Illustrations
Dover Electronic Clip Art

FotoSearch
www.fotosearch.com
Christian Faith Vol. 1, Christian Faith Vol. 2,
Christian Faith Vol. 3

Dreamstime
www.dreamstime.com

Maps used in chapter 2
Adapted from *The Bible Atlas and Companion* published by
Barbour Publishing. Used by permission.

Remaining Tower of Nehemiah, chapter 2
Todd Bolen
www.BiblePlaces.com

Persecuted Christians, chapter 7
Photos courtesy of Gary S. Chapman with
Strategic World Impact
www.swi.org

Wikipedia
Some images have been pulled from various Wikipedia
resources and have been designated as public domain
images because their copyright has expired.

All other images:
iStock Photo, www.istockphoto.com

HISTORY AND MISSION OF THE AMERICAN BIBLE SOCIETY

SINCE THE ESTABLISHMENT OF THE AMERICAN BIBLE SOCIETY IN 1816, ITS HISTORY HAS BEEN CLOSELY INTERTWINED WITH THE HISTORY OF THE NATION WHOSE NAME IT BEARS. IN FACT, THE SOCIETY'S EARLY LEADERSHIP READS LIKE A WHO'S WHO OF PATRIOTS AND OTHER AMERICAN MOVERS AND SHAKERS. ITS FIRST PRESIDENT WAS ELIAS BOUDINOT, FORMERLY THE PRESIDENT OF THE CONTINENTAL CONGRESS. JOHN JAY, JOHN QUINCY ADAMS, DEWITT CLINTON, AND CHRONICLER OF THE NEW NATION JAMES FENIMORE COOPER ALSO PLAYED SIGNIFICANT ROLES IN THE SOCIETY'S HISTORY, AS WOULD RUTHERFORD B. HAYES AND BENJAMIN HARRISON IN LATER GENERATIONS.

From the beginning, the Bible Society's mission has been to respond to the spiritual needs of a fast-growing, diverse population in a rapidly expanding nation. From the new frontier beyond the Appalachian Mountains, missionaries sent back dire reports of towns that did not have a single copy of the Bible to share among its citizens. State and local Bible Societies did not have the resources, network, or capabilities to fill this growing need: a national organization was called for. The ABS committed itself to organizational and technological innovations to meet the demand. No longer subject to British restrictions, the ABS could set up its own printing plants, develop better qualities of paper and ink, and establish a network of colporteurs to get the Bibles to the people who needed them.

Reaching out to diverse audiences has always been at the heart of ABS's mission. Scriptures were made available to Native peoples in their own languages—in Delaware in 1818, followed soon by Mohawk, Seneca, Ojibwa, Cherokee, and others. French and Spanish Bibles were published for the Louisiana Territory, Florida, and the Southwest. By the 1890s the ABS was printing or distributing Scriptures in German, Portuguese, Chinese, Italian, Russian, Danish, Polish, Hungarian, Czech, and other languages to meet the spiritual needs of an increasing immigrant population. In 1836, 75 years before the first Braille Bibles were produced, the ABS was providing Scriptures to the blind in "raised letter" editions.

Responding to the need for Bibles in the languages and formats that speak most deeply to people's hearts continues to be a priority of the ABS. Through its partnerships with other national Bible Societies, the ABS can provide some portion of Scripture in almost any language that has a written form. It has also been able to provide Braille Scriptures for the blind, as well as recorded Scriptures for the visually impaired, dyslexic, and people who have not yet learned to read.

The Bible Society's founders and their successors have always understood the Bible as a text that can speak to people's deepest needs in times of crisis. The ABS distributed its first Scriptures to the military in 1817 when it provided New Testaments to the crew of the USS *John Adams*, a frigate that had served in the War of 1812 and was continuing its service to the country by protecting the American coast from pirates. During the Civil War, the ABS provided Testaments to both northern and southern forces, and it has continued to provide Bibles and Testaments to the U.S. military forces during every subsequent war, conflict, and operation. During the painful post-Reconstruction era, when Jim Crow laws prevailed in many parts of the nation, the ABS was able to provide Scriptures to African Americans through its partnership with the Agency Among Colored People of the South and through the historic Black churches.

This faith that the Word of God speaks in special ways during times of crisis continues to inform the ABS mission. In recent years the Bible Society has produced Scripture booklets addressing the needs of people with HIV/AIDS and of those experiencing profound loss due to acts of terrorism and natural disasters.

Translation and scholarship are key components in the Bible Society's mission of communicating the Word of God faithfully and powerfully. In the mid-20th century, the ABS, in partnership with the United Bible Societies, developed innovative theories and practices of translation. First, they insisted that all the Bible translations they sponsored were to be created exclusively by native speakers, with biblical and linguistic experts serving only as translation consultants to provide technical support and guidance. From the lively and heartfelt translations that resulted, Bible Society scholars were able to see the power of translations that were rendered not on a word-for-word basis, but on a meaning-for-meaning basis that respected the natural rhythms and idioms of the target

languages. This practice of "functional equivalence" translation reinvigorated the practice of translating the Bible into English and is partly responsible for the explosion of new translations of the Bible that have been issued in the past thirty years. These include the Bible Society's own *Good News Translation* and *Contemporary English Version*, but also the *New International Version*, *New Revised Standard Version*, *Today's Century Version*, *New Living Translation*, and *The Message*.

As an organization dedicated to preparing well-researched, faithful translations, the ABS has necessarily committed itself to the pursuit of scholarly excellence. In cooperation with the United Bible Societies, the ABS has helped develop and publish authoritative Greek and Hebrew texts, handbooks on the different books of the Bible, dictionaries, and other technical aids. To make sure that all relevant disciplines are explored, the Bible Society's Nida Institute for Biblical Scholarship convenes symposia and conferences that invite both academic specialists and practicing translators to gather and exchange ideas that will assist translators in communicating the Bible's message to new audiences. For churches and readers seeking a deeper understanding of the Bible and its background, the ABS has developed study Bibles, multimedia video translations with DVD extras, Scriptures in special formats, and website resources.

For almost two centuries the American Bible Society has maintained its commitment to innovation and excellence. While the challenges it has faced over the years have changed, the Society's mission has remained constant—*to make the Bible available to every person in a language and format each can understand and afford, so all people may experience its life-changing message*.

To find out more about the American Bible Society please go to **www.AmericanBible.org** or **Give.AmericanBible.org**